3

Decorating Den Systems, Inc.

SMART & SIMPLE

DECORATING

CREATIVE IDEAS *and* SOLUTIONS
from the Experts *at* Decorating Den Interiors

Carol Donayre Bugg

TIME® LIFE BOOKS

Alexandria, Virginia

TIME-LIFE BOOKS is a division of Time Life Inc.
TIME-LIFE is a trademark of Time Warner Inc. U.S.A.

TIME LIFE INC.
PRESIDENT and CEO: George Artandi

TIME-LIFE CUSTOM PUBLISHING
Vice President and Publisher: Terry Newell
Vice President of Sales and Marketing: Neil Levin
Director of New Product Development: Teresa Graham
Project Coordinator: Jennifer L. Ward
Production Manager: Carolyn Bounds
Quality Assurance Manager: James D. King

Library of Congress Cataloging-in-Publication Data
Bugg, Carol Donayre, date.
    Smart & simple decorating : creative ideas and solutions from the experts at Decorating Den interiors / written by Carol Donayre Bugg.
       p.   cm.
    Includes index.
    ISBN 0-7370-0038-4
    1. Interior decoration. I. Decorating Den Systems. II. Time-Life Books.
  III. Title. IV. Title: Smart and simple decorating.
  NK2110.B84 1999   98-48802
  747—dc21   CIP

Produced by Judd Publishing Inc./Ruina Judd
Designed by Anne Masters Design, Inc./Anne Masters
Edited by Nancy Burke/Burke Associates
Cover room design by Merete Monahan
Cover photograph by Andrew Lautman

First printing.
Printed in the United States

TABLE OF CONTENTS

DEDICATION

For my mentor, partner, and love of my life ... my husband, Jim

INTRODUCTION

The approachable and affordable ideas found in *Smart & Simple Decorating* combine what I have been doing best for thirty years, on my own for the first fifteen years and together with Decorating Den Interiors (DDI) for the last fifteen. "Smart" decorating means creating spaces that have style, dash, and elegance. "Simple" decorating means these environments have to be livable, flexible, and achievable. There may be limits to the size of your home and budget, but there is always something you can do to improve the quality of your surroundings.

To help you get started on decorating the beautiful home you deserve, below are my Seven Keys to Great Decorating.

Seven Keys to Great Decorating

1. **Be a Keen Observer**

If you enjoy going to the movies, window shopping, visiting show-houses and model homes, touring museums, traveling, or reading decorating books and magazines, then you are already on the path to being a keen observer. But now when you do these activities, use them to cultivate your knowledge of interior decorating and increase your awareness of how color and light, line and form, and space and material shape our world.

2. Take an Honest Inventory

The first step in starting any decorating project is taking an objective inventory of what you already own. Assess the furnishings in your rooms the way you seasonally review the clothes in your closet. What can stay and what can go? Get out your camera and take snapshots of your rooms from a variety of angles. The camera never lies. Examine the photos carefully and keep only the furniture and accessories you truly love. Then it's time to draw up a work-in-progress plan.

3. Make a Work-in-Progress Plan

Whatever your time projection for decorating your home—six months, a year, or longer—you need to make a work-in-progress plan and set a series of reasonable goals. A simple, written plan kept in a loose-leaf binder will help you remain on track. Depending on the scope of your decorating project, you may even want to have a binder for each room. Remember that the most workable plans allow for changes and growth in your ever-evolving status and lifestyle, be you single, married, a parent, a grandparent, or an empty nester.

4. Balance Practicality with Panache

The literal meaning for the French word panache is "plume" or "bunch of feathers," especially on a helmet. The helmet has a practical purpose, but visualize how much more dashing the wearer looks and feels when his helmet is decorated with a fanciful plume.

In decorating terms, panache is that personal touch you give the ordinary by turning it into something uniquely your own. Adding fringed shades to an average chandelier, placing a casual wicker rocker next to a prized antique, or daring to paint walls a dramatic blue when everyone else is into beige are all examples of how to personalize your surroundings with your own dash of panache. Best of all, panache does not have to be expensive, and practicality does not have to be mundane.

5. Study the French

Fabulous fakery has always been a part of French design. In fact, the maisons and chateaux of France have been fooling us for centuries with their extraordinary painted *faux* effects and *trompe l'oeil* scenes. *Faux* (pronounced foh) is French for "false" or "counterfeit," as in look-a-like paint finishes including marble (*faux marbre*) and wood (*faux bois*). The *faux* look is also popular for walls, fabrics, and accessories. Literally translated, *trompe l'oeil* (pronounced trop LOY) means "to deceive the eye" and most often describes a finely detailed scene painted on a wall or other surface to create an optical illusion: something that appears to be there—with both depth and solidity—but really isn't.

Both *faux* and *trompe l'oeil* techniques were first found only in the homes of the rich or famous, but their growing popularity has made them accessible to everyone. Many artisans around the country specialize in both techniques and can create with paint almost anything decorative that you can imagine. But beyond custom painting, there are myriad wallpapers and borders that incorporate *trompe* and *faux* techniques—in a vast array of finishes, motifs, and price ranges—and can add beauty and drama to your rooms without breaking your bank account.

6. Give Change a Chance

Giving change a chance requires patience and trust. Often, all a newly decorated room needs to work perfectly is to have something removed that is jarring to the new ambiance: a color that is off, a piece of furniture that no longer belongs, or an accessory that is dated and out of proportion. A strong new color is usually the most striking change one has to get used to in a redecorated room or home, but a different pattern or bolder proportions can also cause concern. Just remember that all change—even for the better—requires a period of adjustment.

7. Remember That the Joy Is in the Doing

Let me put your mind at ease about a few decorating misconceptions. The most common misconception is that because your home is on the small side, or your decorating budget is small, you will not be able to create a luxurious ambiance. Don't allow the constraints of the size of your house or your budget stop you from living beautifully and well. There are decorating schemes, furnishings, and accessories for every situation and for every budget.

And don't let anyone tell you that you have to "start from scratch" to do a great decorating job. Furniture can be reupholstered and repositioned; walls and ceilings can be repainted; hand-me-downs and *objets d'art* can be recycled and showcased in other rooms.

You also don't have to "do it all" when it comes to redecorating your home. Decorating, like life, is an ongoing and evolving work in progress. Start by doing one thing that will revive a tired room, even if you just paint the walls a bolder color.

Finally, throw away the notion that decorating is a luxury. Living in pleasant surroundings is as important for your well-being as is nourishing food for your body.

Samuel Johnson said, "To be happy at home is the ultimate ambition, the end to which every enterprise and labor tends." There are few greater adventures than working to create your dream home. You'll find much joy in deciding on the colors, choosing the fabrics, selecting the furnishings, finding the window treatments, and adding those special finishing touches that will make where you live the most divine place in this world.

1 SPECIAL PLACES

When Decorators Decorate Their Own Homes

You know the feeling you get when you walk into a department store jam-packed with a wide variety of clothing choices? You start by "just looking," hoping to find something original and exciting enough to buy. You try on a few suits and dresses, but nothing seems exactly right. You end up leaving the store with lip gloss and a pair of panty hose, thinking, "A new outfit can wait until I find what I have in mind, even though I'm not quite sure what that is!"

Decorators face a similar dilemma when it comes time to redecorate their own places. They have no problem helping clients make quick decisions about their homes, but some decorators will put off doing anything about their own surroundings, because they are forever on the lookout for the latest, most spectacular idea or solution. And no wonder—they have the inside track. Besides the weekly arrivals of new fabric swatches, wallpaper books, carpet samples, and furniture catalogs, decorators attend trade exhibits and home furnishing shows. How to choose! Of course, most professionals finally do get around to making the right decorating decisions for their homes—and what magnificent choices they come up with!

The following stories illustrate the smart and simple ways some of the decorators at Decorating Den Interiors redesigned their own homes.

Enchanting Eclectic

Coral Gables, Florida, is the home of Decorating Den Interiors decorator Cliff Welles and his wife, Trisha, a real estate attorney. Since purchasing their rambling one-level house in 1983, they have redesigned the entire interior space as well as the outdoor areas.

Initial renovations included redesigning the entryway to reroute traffic flow, expanding and vaulting the family room, replacing the kitchen, and adding a half bath and a screened deck. More recently, they added a master bedroom and included a larger bath and walk-in closet.

Frequent entertainers, Cliff and Trisha enjoy hosting small dinner parties. The open design of the living areas and expanded deck easily accommodate larger affairs as well.

Cliff and Trisha's decorating style is best described as warm, casual, and very personal—with a dash of humor thrown in. The wonderful South Florida climate is an integral part of every renovation detail, inviting views and use of the outdoors. Artifacts and quirky souvenirs from travels in Europe, Africa, and Asia, as well as memorabilia and heirlooms handed down from family on both sides, are all at home together in this uniquely personal residence.

Lending magic, mystery, and merriment to one living room wall (opposite page) is a salvaged chest and an ornately gilded mirror replete with laughing gargoyles, chubby cherubs, and intricate rococo carvings topped by a glittering king-sized crown.

Living Room

With the keen eye of an interior decorator, Cliff saw beyond the original dark and distressed condition of an old chest and saved it from being carted away to the dump. Instead, he gave it new life with a whimsical hand-painted finish, colorful scrolls, and tooling between fairly elaborate doors. According to Cliff, a mirror in a funky and gaudy golden frame seemed a very appropriate partner for the chest.

Cliff and Trisha avoided the obvious furniture arrangement typical of small living rooms by "floating" a pair of angled love seats in the center of the room and leaving the wall space free for bookcases and cabinet units. Burnished finishes on the metal table and the crown molding echo the warm plum and golden hues of the area rug. Individual drapery panels, embellished with matching fringe, are hung high from decorative iron rods, adding height and elegance to the room. Underneath the panels, soft pleated shades filter the afternoon sun.

Cream-colored walls and floor are the backdrop for this sunlit room (right) with white, brown, and muted gold accents. Gold-brown finishes are seen in the coffee table and picture frames. The dark gold drapery panels are hung just below the crown molding to give the room the illusion of greater height.

Dining Area

Moving from the living room to the dining area, we find the table set for a formal sit-down dinner. When entertaining is more casual, however, the chairs are randomly placed out of traffic's way, and the table is pushed up against the wall and set up buffet style.

The dark wood finish of the dining set and the clean lines of the cane-backed chairs continue the warm and airy feel of the living room (above).

Complementing the lush greens outside the glass doors is the earthy mix of warm browns and creams indoors (right). The dark tones of the wood plank table and antique chairs are a perfect contrast to the beige-textured upholstery on the sofas and the cream-colored draperies.

The open and flowing floor plan (below) of this two-bedroom Florida rambler suits the inside/outside entertaining style of the career couple residents.

Family Room

A wraparound deck and 30 linear feet of glass doors invite the wonderful Miami weather into this room. Framing the view are custom draperies with casually swagged valances on a large wooden rod; the effect is to create the feeling of a safari canopy. The finely detailed entertainment center easily houses all of the requisite equipment and also displays collectibles on lighted shelving.

Twin sofas, woven leather side chairs, and a huge multi-purpose ottoman add more variety and texture. For breakfast and casual dining, there is a handsome wood plank, drop-leaf table.

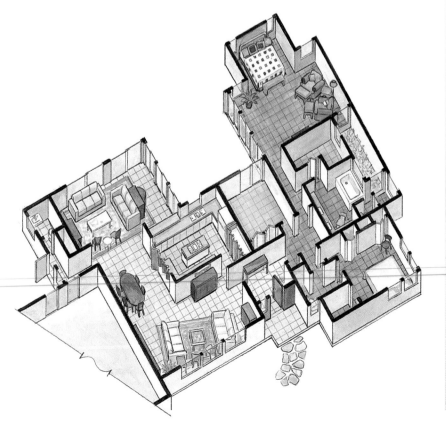

special places 17

This flamboyantly modern bedroom is in striking contrast to the
subtle earthy colors and more
traditional furniture found in the
living areas. Deep green walls
and terra-cotta tiles anchor the
room with a cool, serene feel.

A sumptuously comfortable sitting area makes an inviting spot for intimate conversations, reading, or needlework. The chairs are covered in each of the main colors of the room: bright yellow for the backs, cushions, and ottomans; forest green for the arms and legs; bright yellow-and-wine pillows for accent.

Master Bedroom

If it's true that people's real decorating personality surfaces in their bedroom, then Cliff and Trisha are the "bold and the beautiful." Their master bedroom is a haven in green, with tropical jewel tones, cool terra-cotta tiles, and dramatic bed coverings. To brighten the room with diffused light, soft shades and sheers drape all windows and glass doors, topped by unique quilted valances. The headboard, side table, and bench have been recycled many times, according to Cliff, because they always fit in whatever the decor.

One of the Welles's delicate orchid plants stands in sharp contrast to Ted Kerzie's vibrant painting inspired by the night lights of Los Angeles. A mixture of similarly bright fabrics covers the modern chairs and ottoman.

What a fabulous and inviting home this busy, energetic, and fun-loving career couple have created for themselves and their family and friends.

A Home for all Seasons

Many middle-aged couples have children who have grown up and gone off to college, leaving empty rooms and extra space. Interior decorator Georgia Cox and her husband were determined to convert the somewhat cramped space of their 1970's split-level rambler to accommodate them in this new stage of their lives.

Having available space for remodeling, they seized the chance to expand, customize, and modernize their home.

The Family Room

Georgia's goals for the family room makeover were to expand the space to make it suitable for all kinds of family activities and seasonal changes. She accomplished this with a well-defined plan and the help of an architect.

To maximize their beautiful lake view, Georgia installed a window over the fireplace and replaced an existing window with a glass door that opens on to their lovely redwood deck.

A television is stored in a built-in corner cabinet, and a window seat was created with a built-in sliding unit for stereo and CD storage.

The warm woods of the room contrast beautifully with the textured midnight blue wallcovering. A sectional sofa with contemporary lines, upholstered in a neutral fabric, makes it easy to change the room's accessories for each season.

An oversized window floats in the center of the blue-covered wall, providing the perfect spot for a built-in window seat (opposite). A nearby matching cabinet houses the television and sound system. A colorful collection of books, porcelain vases, and cobalt blue glass adds bright accents throughout the room.

Warm yellows, russets, golds, and browns—with accents of blue and white—predominate this sun-filled family room (left): in the upholstery fabrics, toss pillows, wallcovering, and an assortment of whimsical accessories. A wall of full-length windows provides a bounty of both natural light and nature's beauty. The cobalt blue in the glass collection over the fireplace is echoed in the blue seat cushions, the octagonal-shaped area rug, and in the throw covers.

This split-level floor plan (below) has been adapted to the residents' empty-nester stage, as well as to Georgia's home-based decorating business.

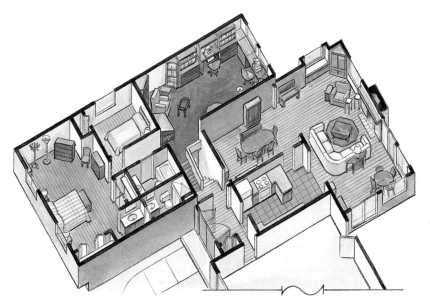

The Home Office

Georgia put her personal signature on her home office (below) with a collection of favorite accent pieces, including an old carpenter's case and an antique drafting table/desk. The office's golds and blues and relaxed, traditional style match the decor in the rest of the home. For a detailed look at Georgia's office, see Part 3.

Georgia does much of her client work from home, and here, in a comfortable corner of the home office, are many of the decorative touches seen in the family room. Cherry wood components provide storage and work space against warm yellow-covered walls. Accents of blue, green, and white are seen in the pottery, plate collection, upholstery, lamps, and throw pillows.

New window treatments, wall-coverings, and a glamorous mix of paisleys, plaids, and small floral prints have revitalized the bedroom (right). Yellows, blues, and greens tie everything together, and wheat-colored walls create a mellow mood.

The Master Bedroom

The Coxes, like many husbands and wives, are as opposite in their tastes and interests as night and day. Georgia describes herself as artistic and her husband, Allen, as analytical, adding, "He is also red-green color blind!"

Working with a builder, Georgia laid out a floor plan for a 13-by-23-foot master suite that provided her and Allen with their own closets, plus a dressing area, vanity, and linen closet.

The new decorating scheme couldn't be too feminine or masculine, and the colors and patterns had to be suitable for one who is color blind. After eliminating fabrics with flowers and stripes, Georgia and Allen decided on plaid, paisley, and small prints in yellow, blue, and green.

All the old furniture was kept, but everything was revived with new fabrics, wallcovering, and rugs.

Instead of a headboard, Georgia created a comfortable backrest by stacking four pillows under a queen-sized bedroll with two quilted shams in front. The bed is covered with a reversible duvet cover—an ideal choice for quick seasonal changes. On the windows, simple valances over two-inch wood blinds smartly solved the need for privacy.

CREATING
Male-Appealing
MASTER BEDROOMS

When redecorating your master bedroom, you may find it hard to choose colors and designs that satisfy both the man and the woman of the house. If so, try some of these gender-friendly tips:

■ Keep floral prints to a minimum.

■ Use a contemporary or impressionistic version of a floral, rather than a traditional bouquet motif.

■ Combine florals with more gender-neutral patterns, such as plaids, chevrons, or stripes.

■ Choose a handsome geometric design.

■ Pick a paisley print.

■ Use solid colors and rely on texture instead of pattern to make a statement.

■ Select simple, tailored treatments for beds and windows.

■ Paint or paper the room in deep, rich jewel tones rather than in soft pastels.

Texas Interpretation of Victorian

Cathy Buchanan describes her home as "neo-Victorian in a modern subdivision." As a lover of antiques and of the romance of the Victorian era, Cathy was prepared to reinterpret this gracious period to suit the Buchanans' contemporary way of life.

Victorian style incorporates furniture and accessories from all periods of the past. Thus the charm of Victorian rooms, then and now, lies in the eclectic mixing of furnishings and accessories in a wide variety of styles.

What ties Cathy's home to the Victorian era is her choice of deep, rich colors, exuberant patterns, graceful swags and jabots, and luxurious passementerie (ornamental edgings and trimmings). What keeps her home from being a mere replication of Victorian style is Cathy's contemporary adaptations for how the Buchanans live now.

Finally, because the Buchanan floor plan, as in many homes, allows one to see both the living room and the dining room as you enter, Cathy had to carefully coordinate the flow of color and design throughout her home.

The Foyer

With a decorator's sense of the dramatic, Cathy turned her foyer into a stunningly grand entryway by covering the walls in a blue and white striped moiré wallpaper accented with glittering, gold stripes.

New honey-toned *faux* wood flooring replaces the foyer's old ceramic tiling, and a pale taupe, short loop-and-pile carpet brightens the once gloomy stairwell that faces the entrance. A handsome kilim—placed at an angle on the entryway floor— adds an extra dash of drama.

This striking foyer is also host to a collection of five hand-painted engravings of blue and white, nineteenth-century porcelain plates with gold accents.

Blue-, white-, and gold-striped moiré wallpaper serves as a brilliant disguise for this foyer's peculiar angles and asymmetry and visually adds height to the eight-foot ceiling (opposite).

The Living Room

The challenges Cathy faced with her living room included low ceilings, wood-toned block paneling, low light levels, her existing furniture, and a dark blue oriental rug with peachy-beige and off-white accents running through the design. Painting the paneling, often a good solution, was not an option here. As Cathy confided, "This was the only decorating preference my husband ever expressed!"

She came up with a plan that included reupholstering the sofa and her two wing chairs, purchasing two new Georgian-style armchairs, and designing new window treatments.

The elegant lines of Cathy's sofa were enhanced with a lovely new bisque damask covering and a newer-looking deeper dressmaker skirt. She picked a flirty tassel tapestry for her old chairs and a cheery plaid for the new pair, both in colors that blended with the oriental rug and picked up the dining room scheme.

Cathy's intricate window design called for swags and cascades that drip gold bullion fringe, plus off-center panels tied back, high and low, over floor-length voile sheers. One panel on each window is floor-length, and the other two panels pool softly on the floor; all are hung from an antique gold cus-

tom rod. Asymmetrical window treatments in an alabaster moiré, reminiscent of early nineteenth-century draperies, now flank the handsome brick fireplace.

The mood of the Victorian theme in Cathy's living room was relaxed by introducing neutrals and textures and using dark colors and strong patterns as accents. "By adding off-white in large amounts and introducing blue as a counterpoint to the yellow-orange-toned wood paneling," said Cathy, "the room has a lighter, softer, richer look, suitable for entertaining—or just relaxing with a very pleased husband."

The richly deep tones of the wood paneling make a perfect backdrop for the exquisite lines of the bisque, damask-covered sofa (left). Leather-bound books, glittering candlesticks, potted plants, and heirloom porcelain pieces complete the elegant assemblage.

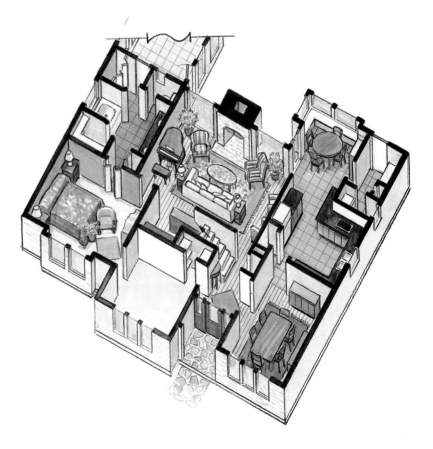

The owner's eye for color maintains harmony and consistency throughout the connecting rooms of her neo-Victorian Texas home (right).

After. Creamy bisque and alabaster colors open up the room (left). New Georgian chairs, covered in a neutral check, face the couch. The oriental rug now blends perfectly with the draperies and furniture.

The old wing chairs were moved to one end of the room, forming an intimate conversation nook. (above). An elegantly curved alabaster urn underscores the new, light color and feel of the redesigned room and softly suggests the deep curves of the alabaster draperies.

Before. The old living room was dark and unappealing (left). The wing chairs were languishing in outdated upholstery, and a beautiful oriental rug was lost among the clutter of furniture.

The Master Bedroom

Remove either the intense color on the walls or the vibrant pattern of the fabric and the Buchanan's master bedroom would not be nearly as striking. It is the combination of these two design elements that makes the once-dull space come alive.

When Cathy turned to her master bedroom, more challenges arose to test her imagination. First she fell in love with a closeout fabric—the last bolt of a discontinued fabric design. Fifty-seven yards of fabric was all Cathy was able to buy. Usually a decorator designs a treatment before figuring how much yardage is

Before. This bedroom is best described as dull and neglected.

After. Deep emerald walls are trimmed with white molding. A richly colored Victorian fabric drapes over the four-poster, covers the bed, and curves along the window. Three stacked hatboxes are cleverly used as a side table.

required. In this case, Cathy had to reverse the procedure.

Her next challenge was to install a swagged canopy treatment over her pine bed, even though the bed had no supports for a full canopy. She achieved her task by swagging a half-inch trim cord across rails covered in gathered wine fabric. The cor-

ners of the four pencil posts were then draped with generous bishoped-panels accented with tassels. A quilted coverlet, envelope pillow shams, and wine dust ruffle completed the luxurious bed setting.

For her box bay window, Cathy created the look of contrasting "fans" between the swags with standard cone jabots, pulled up at the side and pinned to the flanking swags.

White shutters and trim, together with the new, pale cut-pile-and-loop carpet, added contrast to the overall rich emerald and burgundy scheme.

Cathy faced one last challenge when the new lamps arrived. The color wasn't right. So, she repainted them.

It was Cathy's treatment of color and pattern that made the room she once described as "totally without oomph" into a treasured oasis.

By contrasting variations of the deep, rich colors she loves with light accents and warm wood tones, Cathy created a pleasing, "lite-Victorian" ambiance for the whole Buchanan house.

Re-creating VICTORIANA

If you would like to try re-creating Victoriana in your home, consider using one or more of these classic Victorian elements.

- Eclectic mixes of furniture and accessories influenced by the Gothic, Rococo, Romanesque, and Greek revival periods, with ornate detailing and curvaceous lines.

- Large-patterned wall–coverings, stenciled walls, and deep frieze borders.

- Window treatments utilizing swags, jabots, and cascades of velvet, silk, or lace, finished with passementerie (ornamental trims, tassels, and fringes).

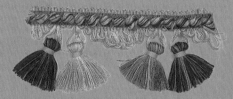

- Rich, dark, jewel tones—garnet, antique gold, sapphire—for walls, carpets, draperies, and upholstery.

- Hardwood floors layered with oriental rugs.

- Decorative accessories such as marble tables, spool-turned legs, bentwood furniture, brass beds, pressed-tin ceilings, globed gaslights, and palm trees.

2 BEAUTIFUL SPACES

Inside Decorator Showhouses and Model Homes

My interest in model home decorating has a long history, beginning with childhood visits to the model house built inside Manhattan's landmark furniture store store, W & J Sloane. Eventually a career in design led me to owning my own model home interior decorating business.

I still decorate models today, but as Director of Design for Decorating Den Interiors (DDI), the scope of the projects has broadened considerably. On almost any day, you can find a group of DDI decorators working on model homes or showhouses somewhere in North America.

At other times, Decorating Den Interiors is involved in projects with more national visibility, such as our association with *LIFE* magazine as the decorators of their 1994 American Dream House, designed by Robert A. M. Stern, Architects. DDI was also given the plum role of decorating one of a dozen rooms for the first showhouse ever undertaken by the PBS television series *This Old House.*

On the following pages, without leaving your own home, you will take a grand tour of the media room for *This Old House,* the *LIFE* American Dream House, and an array of smart and simply decorated rooms from coast to coast and across Canada.

The Media Room
for the *This Old House* Showhouse

When Decorating Den Interiors was asked to decorate the media room for the first showhouse featured on PBS's *This Old House,* we were faced with a cross between a model and a showhouse. The building had a history dating back to 1720, but with less than a dozen rooms, it could hardly be considered a mansion. The line between model and showhouse was further blurred because DDI's media room was under construction, which meant we had to work from blueprints.

Decorating Den Interiors' good fortune was that the Milton, Massachusetts, location of the *This Old House* project was literally in the backyard of one our longtime franchise partners and regional directors, Anne Fawcett. Five months before the filming deadline, Anne and I met at the site to get a feel for the project. Afterward, we exchanged ideas. Anne and her team of decorators, craftspeople, and installers then worked together to create what turned out to fit everyone's standards of a "favorite" room.

Our vision for marrying a new media room with this historic old home was to pair the latest in modern technology with the best of classic traditional design.

The decorating plan began with a color palette of paprika and honey combined with spruce green. Texture was the next important design element: Soft chenille, antiqued leather, painted metals, smooth glass, grained woods, and woven wicker all came together for a comfortable and family-friendly environment.

Walls upholstered in raw silk, floors carpeted in wool Berber, windows draped with multilayered treatments, and shelves filled with books helped enhance the room's acoustical quality—a key ingredient of a state-of-the-art media room.

A curved-back sofa was placed diagonally not only to allow the proper distance from a large-screen television, but also to route traffic through the room. Two chairs—one in leather, the other in cushioned wicker—offered additional seating. Behind the sofa, creating a private space for writing or reading, is a glass and metal desk and a handsome iron chair.

The lighting mood was set by a mélange of decorative halogen lamps illuminating the hand-painted ceiling, which is reminiscent of old neighborhood movie theaters.

Showhouses, Models, AND Homeramas

■ **Showhouse.** A mansion or historic home where each room shows off the talents of different interior decorators. The purpose of a showhouse, which is usually open for a month, is to raise funds for a local charity.

■ **Model Home.** One or more decorated homes set aside in an individual builder's subdivision as a display of the different floorplans available. These models remain open until the project is sold out.

■ **Parade of Homes/Homerama.** Events in certain areas of the country where a dozen or so builders each construct a sample house that defines their unique workmanship. The public is invited to visit these decorated homes for a limited time.

Behind the angled sofa, a library wall of books and a glass-topped desk on a lovely iron base create an intimate nook for reading, writing, or meditating (opposite).

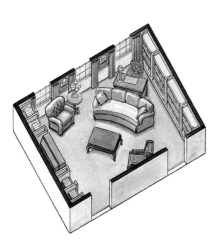

This floor plan (above) shows how a small space can be transformed into a marvelous multipurpose room, complete with good traffic flow and several clearly defined areas.

Colorful accents of mellow honey and glittery gold are found throughout the media room: from the bamboo shades, oversized toss pillow, and matching throw to the ornamental pears, the trim on the coffee table, and the elaborate, multitiered lamp.

Artist Julie Williams painted bees, butterflies, and small animals within a geometric border on the ceiling and then aged it all with an antique glaze (below).

In an adjoining powder room (above) artist Nancy Erving picked up the media room palette and painted the walls with finely detailed monkeys and palm trees in chinoiserie fashion.

Canadian Cancer Society Benefit Showhouse

Two Decorating Den Interiors' design firms pooled their expertise to produce a splendid dining room for a showhouse benefiting the Canadian Cancer Society.

Their approach was to design a room with a gardenlike setting suitable for grand parties or for Sunday brunches. They "flowered" the room in hues of brilliant hibiscus red and lush apple green, gently mellowed with soft neutrals.

Other enchanting details delight the eye and soul: a wrought-iron table covered in a delicate sheer that floats on the faded oriental rug; exquisite drapery panels that add stature to the window; and an irresistible balloon-design chandelier.

Opposites attract in the decorative combination of light, airy wood side chairs and stately upholstered ones. Note the graceful skirts and simple brass buttons down the back of the upholstered pair.

As delightfully inviting as a gracious hostess, this charming dining room beckons one to feast in the most resplendent of fashions.

Upholstered host chairs (right) covered in a hibiscus red brocade, set the color and style for this enchanting dining room— a sophisticated blend of traditional furniture pieces.

Chair seats covered in rose-and-cream stripes (opposite) blend beautifully with the solid colored host chairs and echo the pattern in the draperies. The muted creams and pinks in the oriental rug perfectly complement the neutral-toned wood furniture.

The Orchestra London and the John Gordon Home
London, Ontario, Canada

In choosing to showcase the John Gordon Home instead of one of the typical mansions selected in the past, the Orchestra London saw it as an opportunity of mutual benefit, both for the people who lived at the John Gordon Home and for the community who depended on its services.

The John Gordon Home is a continuum of care model for people living with AIDS and HIV. Decorating the living room and kitchen of the Home was a project very close to the heart of Canadian decorator Carole Andrews. She had learned firsthand the full meaning of the Home's love, support, and caregiving when her son was a resident there before his passing away.

Earthy browns, beiges, and golds in a variety of textures and patterns make the living room a warm and comfortable haven. The stunning window treatment—an intricate mix of contrasting-colored swags, gathered plaid draperies, linen-look shades, and soft, white sheers—is the room's dramatic focal point.

The Living Room

Carole explains her approach to revamping the Home's living room: "My goal when planning this room was to create an environment filled with warmth, aspects of nature, and a variety of textures. I chose to envision a room that my son would have enjoyed. He had a sense of elegance and style and an appreciation for beauty and comfort."

The dramatic window treatment, with its asymmetrical layering of valances, swags, sheers, blinds, and draperies, became the living room's focal point. An unusual application of a laser-cut border to the ceiling overlaps onto the warm caramel-colored walls. Carole had the existing furnishings refinished and re-covered in warm neutral tones. But for the rug, throw pillows, and draperies, she used vibrantly colorful plaid and leopard patterns in a variety of textures that mixed well together. As a final touch, Carole positioned a painted screen and a small, indoor waterfall pond to separate the living room from the kitchen area.

The Kitchen

In the kitchen of the John Gordon Home, natural birch wood is used throughout for cabinets and drawers. A pair of curved, stainless steel cabinet doors over the sink added a modern touch, and recycled steel mesh doors below a work station were an environmentally practical addition. The sink was set into the corner with one wide cabinet door beneath. When a resident becomes wheelchair-bound, the cabinet door can be removed to allow easy access to the sink.

How satisfying it is to work on a showhouse project that will benefit others for years to come.

Clean lines, open spaces, neutral colors, and maximum accessibility to cabinets and drawers are integral to this kitchen's redesign. They not only make for a charming, contemporary-style kitchen, but provide easy access to utensils and work tops for residents who are wheelchair-bound.

Burlington, Vermont, YWCA Showhouse

A mansion in downtown Burlington, Vermont, was the site of the local YWCA's first annual "Decorator Showcase House." The DDI team working on this project chose a stylish color scheme for the living room, featuring luscious plum-painted walls and glazed, gold-leaf moldings. To hide the less than desirable window views, the decorators used an array of antique buckles to pull handkerchief swags and soft window sheers into graceful folds over each window. One decorator's adorable Labrador retriever naps on a wing chair, epitomizing the relaxed feeling of the room.

In stunning contrast to the plum-colored walls is the abundance of layer upon layer of sheer, white draperies cascading softly into gathers on the floor. Plum-patterned handkerchief swags top the panels and match the tableskirt on the round occasional table.

Decorating the *LIFE* Dream House

LIFE magazine's award-winning 1994 Dream House, designed by Robert A. M. Stern, Architects, wasn't constructed until the spring of 1996. It was then that Stern's shingle-style design was built in a planned community near Atlanta, Georgia, modeled after small-town America. The neighborhood was an ideal setting for a house with such old-fashioned characteristics.

The same deference to timeless appeal and concern for affordability that *LIFE* magazine had required from the architect also guided DDI decorators Terri Ervin, Judith Slaughter, and me in designing the interiors.

Natural-toned walls and floors, warm red plaids, red and green solids, and black and white accents tie together all the decorative elements of this spacious great room. A sisal area rug, bordered in a geometric pattern, delineates the dining area from the living space.

The Great Room

Rather than walls dividing spaces (as in much older houses), the open-plan living and dining areas in the *LIFE* house are visually defined by two similarly stenciled sisal rugs. Each space conveys an aura of relaxed elegance, aptly suited for today's more informal lifestyles.

The dining area's handsome light wood oval table and chairs, together with a pair of plaid host chairs, can easily accommodate both everyday meals and elegant entertaining.

Soft yellow walls and a bright white tray ceiling and trim light up the spacious 18-by-27-foot great room. Intimate arrangements of generously proportioned upholstered pieces in mellow reds and greens are gathered invitingly around the classic fireplace.

A variety of new accessories with old-time appeal complements the selection of wicker and wood tables and chairs. Accents of black, as in the simple roman shades, add contrast and a touch of sophistication.

Breakfast Area

The spirit of the past lives on in the Dream House's breakfast nook. Breezy window treatments filter the early morning light, creating a cozy atmosphere for breakfast. A built-in banquette, covered with striped cushions and pretty pillows, surrounds a marble-topped table with a wrought-iron base.

This delightful breakfast nook (below) features a banquette cushioned in beige and dark green stripes. The window valances are patterned in a complementing beige and green vegetable print.

An oversized armchair and matching ottoman (left) are covered with the same red plaid used on the dining chairs. Yellow walls are topped by a white tray ceiling. A sisal rug, black roman shades, and white window trim are striking accents.

The Den

Decorated in a marvelous mix of maple, red, and sage colors, and corduroy and cotton fabrics, the den is an intimate space reserved for playing, reading, or working at the built-in desk.

The den (left) is a mellow mix of warm tones, textures, and wood furniture. The sofa is covered in gold corduroy with contrasting dark piping. Walls are painted a soft gold above the chair rail and a dark sage green beneath. Wicker baskets filled with greenery complete the peaceful picture.

On one wall of the den—providing a perfect spot for paying bills or catching up with correspond-ence—is a built-in desk with deep storage shelves (above). Both are painted in dark sage green and accessorized with a collection of old clocks and leather-bound books.

THE PLEASURES OF Plaid

The geometric box plan of inter-secting horizontal and vertical lines and colors makes plaid a perennial favorite as a stand-alone or go-with-all decorative fabric. Plaid mixes well with other textile pat-terns, and it can serve as a road map for choosing a room's color scheme. The addition of plaid accents and accessories can also "relax" a formal room. Among the many other advantages of decorat-ing with plaid are its:

■ **Universal Appeal:** Whether Scottish tar-tan, Provincial print, Thai silk, or American wool, plaid speaks a universal language.

■ **Timelessness:** Plaid is always in style and forever fashionable.

■ **Agelessness:** Plaid is both youthful and old-worldly, as appealing in a child's bedroom as it is in the living room.

■ **Gender Friendliness:** Most men and women love plaid.

■ **Endless Variations:** Plaid designs are unlimited when it comes to scale and color combinations.

Upstairs Hallway

On the red harlequin-papered second-floor landing is a table that former president Jimmy Carter built for his wife, Rosalind, to use while teaching her Sunday school classes in Plains, Georgia. All proceeds from the public tours of the *LIFE* house went to both The Children's Center in Atlanta and one of the Carters' and Decorating Den Interiors' favorite charities—Habitat for Humanity International.

Master Bedroom

Another sensible bow to the '90s is the master bedroom's location on the main floor. Sensual pale sage walls and ecru textured sheers envelop a simple pencil post bed facing away from the outside world. The subdued prints and textures of the chaise, tufted ottoman, graceful tableskirt, and pillows cast this private space under a romantic spell.

Boy's Bedroom

Crisp navy and white stripes set a pleasant background for a boy's room. The nautical theme is complemented by the navy plaid on the bed.

Below the chair rail (right), the walls are painted a contrasting deep ecru. The handmade side table is finished in the same dark tones as the floor.

This young boy's bedroom (above) is decorated in traditional nautical colors. Deep navy accents coordinate with the wallpaper and plaid bedspread. Nautical accessories abound, including framed prints of tall ships and assorted model schooners and sailboats.

Subtle colors and sumptuous comfort are the hallmarks of this romantic bedroom (right). Sage green walls and ceiling are trimmed with white molding. The bed is beautifully dressed with cream and green spreads and pillows.

Putting the Personality in a Model Home

During the first visit to customers' homes, the decorators at Decorating Den Interiors have the opportunity to learn about their clients' lifestyles, needs, and desires.

There is no such opportunity when decorating model homes. A decorator has to imagine who will be living there, give that future prospect a personality, and then decorate the model home accordingly. Budgets and deadlines are notoriously tight, so the decorator has to create a knockout image for little money and in record time.

Carol Stearns rates high in both areas. For the cabana/guest house of a model home in a prestigious Florida golf course community, she devised a bright and lively theme that cost little but thrilled visitors.

Carol's choice of bright yellow walls set the cabana mood. The petite tufted love seat is new, but the dresser, nightstands, rattan chair, and lamps were recycled from a previous model home. Inexpensive plaid and solid fabrics were chosen to dress the bed, and two-inch white wood blinds covered the windows. Flea market shopping produced the darling birdhouses.

Bright reds and yellows, plaids and prints, whimsical accessories and old-fashioned comfort are the highlights of this cabana/guest house in a large Florida home. Creamy yellow walls make a subtle backdrop for the bright bedspread, buttoned pillows, and red upholstered love seat.

Ideas Worth Copying

Making the most of a slim budget and a tight space can produce some ingenious results. Such was the case when Carol Stearns was asked to decorate another model home. Thankfully, her builder's signature cabinets and mirrors did not have to come out of her budget.

A couple of antiquing trips produced a set of six chairs and a wrought-iron table base, but two of the chairs were damaged and had different colored seats. Not a problem for Carol! She purposely set apart the chairs from their mates with white quilted slipcovers.

A moss green and purple floral pattern was selected for the swag and shirred cascades, which gracefully follow the line of the window. Coordinating fringe and white sheers enriched the treatment. The tawny sisal rug bordered in black added texture and definition.

Model home decorators are often accused of using mirrors and glass to make spaces look deceptively larger. In reality, they create the most visually impressive space possible—no matter the size of the room or the budget. When mirrors and glass work as well as they do in this dining room, they're a trick worth emulating.

The artful use of mirrors has visually doubled the size of this dining room and given it depth, beauty, and sophistication. A glass tabletop seems to float in midair and contributes to the open feeling of the room. Colors are neutral throughout, with bright white accents providing contrast and light.

Unforgettable Model Homes...
In Record Time!

Unusual ideas for dressing windows are Indiana decorator Karen Kappus's way of making a statement that is hard to forget. The striking sage and cream tent treatment was designed to open up the room, draw attention to the architectural feature of the raised ceiling, and enhance the spectacular view of the golf course.

The good news about this deceptively simple window treatment is that it requires a minimum of fabric. Here, Karen combined two relatively inexpensive fabrics, a stripe with a solid, for maximum impact.

The bad news is that this unique treatment requires the tools of the trade of three different professionals: first, a decorator to give the correct proportions and scale, along with accurate measurements; next, a drapery workroom specialist to carry out the design and fabricate the finished product; and last, the person who will make the first two look good—a skilled installer.

A floral tableskirt picks up the red of the chairs and the sage green in the cushions (above). Apple-adorned wooden stools add a whimsical accent. Rattan chairs painted a deep red are accented with cushions covered in a sage green that matches the walls and window trim.

On a different model home project, Karen designed another unforgettable window treatment for a charming country kitchen. Once again it was important to frame the window and expose the pleasant view, but this time it was also necessary to add softness and curves to a very square room. Notice how the face of the red plaid changes depending on whether it is folded, draped, shirred, or laid flat, illustrating how you can create different results with the same fabric.

The awning effect curves softly out from the walls. Gentle arches enhance the small transoms, while the folds and curves at the top add depth and detail. Purple piping trims the valance and drapery panels. A timeless fleur-de-lis pattern dots the textured green wallpaper and is repeated on the scalloped collar embellishment. With the addition of the whimsical hot air balloon, Karen adds one more smashing detail to stir a prospective buyer's memory.

The dining area of this kitchen is wonderfully lit by a wall of windows draped and valanced in a red plaid trimmed with purple (below). Lilac-colored birdcages pick up the purple in the drapery and are a delightful addition to the rustic look (bottom).

Intimations of a Bygone Era

Decorating Den Interiors' decorators Cathi Lloyd and Linda Starcevich were asked to breathe life into a local builder's empty model home. Being one house among a Parade of Homes, it was up to Cathi and Linda to make this model stand above the rest. At the request of the builder's wife, the home had to have a casual, understated elegance reminiscent of a bygone era.

This country kitchen (above) is a delightful blend of various wood finishes and furniture styles that mix together marvelously. Adding pattern and panache is an old-fashioned wallcovering depicting country scenes in cherry and cream colors—a perfect complement to the built-in cherry wood cabinets.

Dining Room

Old-world charm characterizes the small, but inviting, dining room with its burnished wood tones and rich green and gold accents. The window is dressed in two coordinating prints—a stripe and an acanthus leaf design.

The added height of the drapery and the custom-stenciled gold pattern cleverly painted along the ceiling line draw your eyes to the upper wall and above.

Traditional furniture and elegant, gold-accented accessories characterize this European-style dining room (left). The parchment-colored wallpaper dramatically contrasts with the dark wood furniture. Hand-stenciled along the ceiling edge and upper wall is a lovely, gold fleur-de-lis pattern.

Kitchen

Following European tradition, the kitchen uses a variety of wood finishes; and while they all don't "match," they definitely go together. The handsome dark cherry wood cabinets warmly complement the charming red and white toile wallcovering selected by the decorators. Over the generous window is a simple combination toile valance and plaid cornice.

The breakfast area is defined by a black oval area rug. Above the light cherry wood kitchen table hangs a verdigris chandelier capped with smart black shades.

American Dream Home...
Mediterranean-Style

A buttery yellow carpet over "marble-look" floor tiles is the anchoring element amid this mix of floral patterns and gold-toned wood. Contrasting black accents are seen in the wrought-iron railings and tables.

A builder/decorator "dream team" designed this European-fashioned model for a Pensacola Parade of Homes. Nancy Travis and Linda Dean worked closely with builder David Miller to present the public with a home that has the charm and sensuality of the Mediterranean but is still suitable for a carefree Florida lifestyle.

Foyer and Great Room

The sunlit and airy expanse of the spacious great room, the "marble-look" floor tiles, and the eclectic mixture of furnishings in muted golden tones promote a European ambiance. To make the entrance and foyer more fitting for such a grand setting, the decorators suggested something different from the traditional wood entrance railing. The new and exquisite custom-wrought-iron railing makes a gracious bridge between the Old World and modern Florida.

Kitchen

In the kitchen, combining a tin ceiling and Corian countertops extends the American-Euro style found in the foyer and great room. And the use of the same "marble-look" floor tiles first seen in the great room continues the home's spacious and light feeling.

The curves and softness of the balloon valances are pleasing counterpoints to the straight lines of the cabinets and striped wallcovering.

Muted gold colors with white and black accents are seen throughout the kitchen and eating area (above). Soft golden cabinets are contrasted with white countertops and black appliances. A striped, gold and off-white wallpaper pattern blends beautifully with the cabinets and neutral-colored, tiled floor.

Small in size but rich in dramatic detailing, this sunlit, airy bedroom has the look and feel of a tropical island hideaway. Floor-to-ceiling windows flood the space with natural light; soft, flowing white fabrics on the bed and windows cool the room and add a touch of serenity.

Adding Glamour and Space to a Small Bedroom

The usual approach to a small bedroom is to downplay the bed, but decorator Laura Bowman-Messick chose the opposite approach and made an impressive iron grapevine canopy bed the center of attention. Drawing one's eyes to the bed takes the focus off the size of the room.

Laura contrasted this dramatic focal point with understated bed coverings and draperies, keeping them natural, soft, and flowing. The window treatments, featuring tab-tops, can be drawn at night for privacy and opened during the day for a view of the golf course.

Laura also didn't cut back on the scale of the room's other furniture and accessories: a trunk, chair, and ottoman. The wallpaper border in a ribbon design runs around the room, while the floor is accented with a deep wool shag rug.

What this intimate bedroom suite lacks in size, it certainly makes up for in glamour.

Creating a "Model" Bedroom for New Owners

There is yet another scenario associated with decorating model homes. Fifteen years ago, when I was working with builders, the models were never sold until the entire project was completed and all of the houses were occupied. However, when some developers build a model house for a Homerama or a Parade of Homes, their goal is to sell that model—and as quickly as possible.

With less than a month until the builder's grand opening, Indiana decorator Gail Romaine was still confident that she could meet the deadline. At that point, she had the freedom to choose any materials and furnishings that were immediately accessible. Then a few weeks into the project, the builder was fortunate enough to sell his house to people moving to Indiana.

Literally overnight, Gail's plans changed and she had to deal with an out-of-state client. Where colors and patterns were concerned, new decisions that suited the client had to be made quickly.

For one thing, window treatments now needed to be functional as well as decorative, since people would be living there. Gail used shades for privacy, but for panache she added lace with tab-top fabric detailing hung over antique brass rods.

A plump duvet cover and matching shams, in a luscious grape-and-vine pattern banded in burgundy, were chosen for the vintage looking iron and carved wood bed. Placed in front of the recessed bay window area, the four-poster bed makes quite a visual statement.

A four-poster, iron-and-wood bed is the focal point of this master bedroom. Deep purples and greens color the intricate, grape-and-vine pattern of the duvet cover and pillow shams. White lace draperies keep the feel of the room light and airy.

Colorful Teen Retreat

Janice Stagg took a slightly different approach when it came to decorating this particular room in a builder's model. Having a teenage daughter in need of her own new bedroom furnishings, she decided to involve her in the design process. Then later, when the house was sold, her daughter would have the things Janice had specified for the model to update her own room.

To start with, Janice redesigned the bed that her daughter's grandfather had fashioned for the child when she was only two. Now it was transformed into a more suitable daybed with the addition of a sophisticated duvet cover accented by bright, contemporary-style toss pillows. The four horizontally joined posts of the bed and their top, canopy area were left unadorned, giving a sleek and open appearance to the room. The wooden posts were also finished in the same warm, russet tones as the chest of drawers.

As a decorating theme, mother and daughter honed in on the family cat. The redesigned bed was cleverly accented with tree branches, birdhouses, birds, and—of course—stuffed cats. A whimsical "kitty kat" pattern was chosen as one of the prints for the collage of fabrics on the chair, as well as for the pillows and the pegged-top valance. A striped multicolor area rug, placed diagonally to the bed, echoes the bright reds and golds in the pillows, upholstery, and valance.

All the brilliant colors in the fabrics and rug are nicely relieved by the snow-white duvet cover and white pleated shades. Neutral walls were given an extra bit of punch with a harlequin design created by running narrow ribbon on the diagonal and holding it in place with upholstery tacks. A smaller version of the diamond motif is repeated on a bold aubergine and yellow pillow.

The builder sold his model, the daughter has a sensational new bedroom, and Janice had the satisfaction of pleasing two people.

The handmade canopy bed has been pared down to its original redwood finish and turned into a sophisticated daybed with white duvet, brightly colored pillows, and a collection of stuffed cats. Red, aubergine, yellow, blue, and green are mixed, matched, and contrasted in a montage of solid and patterned fabrics.

UPHOLSTERY
Collage

To inject personality into your upholstered pieces, mix prints on the arms, backs, and seats.

For upholstered pieces, such as sofas, love seats, and chairs, remember the following guidelines:

■ Cover the frame in a solid and the seat and back cushions in a print on top only. Then you can reverse the cushions for a solid look.

■ Using three coordinating fabrics, cover arms with one, back and front with the second, and seat cushions with the third.

■ With a monochromatic color scheme, try mixing textures: leather and tweed for a casual look; damask and silk for a formal air.

For dining or occasional chairs, try these tips:

■ Cover the front in a solid or print, the back in a check or plaid.

■ Cover the seat in a solid, and wrap the back in a different solid or coordinating stripe.

■ Alternate fabrics on individual dining chairs.

3 RAVISHING ROOMS

Decorating Room By Room

Decorating Den Interiors' mission statement is: "Making the world more beautiful, one room at a time." Showing a variety of approaches to individual situations, the new creations shown on the following pages exemplify what all our interior decorators strive to achieve with their clients.

Sometimes a job calls for a total makeover, but more often than not, a few changes will make a stale room look and feel fresh. These changes might include: rearranging furniture pieces into a more pleasing conversational grouping; getting rid of a long-detested item and treating yourself to something beautiful; replacing dull and faded fabrics with new colors and patterns; or giving away an item from your old matching suite of furniture and replacing it with something totally different. In the dining room this might be upholstered chairs; in the living room it may be an iron-and-glass coffee table; and in the bedroom it could be the most romantic bed you can find.

Without the "Before" pictures on the following pages, you wouldn't realize just how far these rooms have come from their original humble beginnings. Even the rooms that got off to terribly bad starts or had to be decorated from scratch, now sparkle and shine.

The secret behind these magical transformations is the ability of the decorators to guide their clients' ideas to the most direct and pleasing conclusion. Turn the page and see for yourself!

Living Rooms

Does your living room live up to its name, or has it lost its vitality through benign neglect and inactivity? Perhaps you have even designated your living room "off limits," reserving it for company only.

Today's living rooms are multipurpose spaces designed for the enjoyment of a variety of activities by children and parents, friends and guests. Most importantly, a living room should manifest "life" by being thoroughly "lived in" every day.

Minnesota Casual

In the case of a vibrant, young Minneapolis family, it was time to introduce a warmer feeling to the cold, white rooms of their 1950s rambler. Their first decision was to retire their family hand-me-downs and redecorate the room in colors, patterns, and textures that better reflected their lifestyle.

Since the couple preferred an intimate approach to entertaining, a single conversational grouping of furniture became the focal point, and overscaled upholstered pieces were angled to face each other.

For color, the couple chose an autumnal palette. The love seats were covered in a deep terra-cotta chenille, and the two oversized armchairs were upholstered in a bold, fall-inspired plaid. The painted walls were deepened to a rich, sage green and topped by off-white trim to keep the room from appearing too dark. The simple, but classic window treatment combined wood blinds under butterscotch panels.

A handsome wood, glass, and iron coffee table rests on the black-bordered rug. Earthy accessories play well alongside contemporary lighting elements, and the mantel holds a display of arts-and-crafts pieces in muted earthy tones.

Against a soothing canvas of sage green walls (opposite page), two armchairs covered in gold, russet, blue, green, and wine plaid flank the fireplace. Hand-crafted objects in autumnal colors adorn the mantelpiece, side table, and coffee table.

After. The long expanse of window (left), with its lovely outdoor view and abundant sunlight, is draped in soft, butterscotch panels that reflect the natural light and contrast subtly with the green walls. White wood blinds filter the sun and provide privacy.

Before. Plain white walls, few accessories, and inadequate lighting add to the unfriendly look of this room (above).

Tricks of the Trade

The real trick in card playing is to win with the hand one is dealt. There is a parallel in decorating.

Unfortunately, most people believe that the only way to redecorate a room is to throw everything out and start from scratch. Not so. Making the best out of what one has to work with is the strategy Jan Tomlinson followed in redecorating her own Texas ranch house, starting with the living room.

The most obvious change to Jan's living room is her skilled transformation of the sofa and love seat. They went from dowdy to dandy with their new taupe tone-on-tone cotton fabric, but they really became divine when Jan skirted the pieces in luxurious bullion fringe.

Not until you study the differences between the "Before" and "After" pictures do you discover her other subtle moves: Jan gave a jaunty angle to the mahogany cocktail table; she added a mottled texture to the ceiling while keeping the walls light. Window treatments were designed to be simple and airy, with iron rods and finials complementing the many other metal accents in the room.

A mix of patterns from the stunning area rug, afghan, paisley pillows, and tableskirt warms up the otherwise neutral palette.

Before. A lack of color, texture, and variety, with no unifying theme to pull the room together, results in an outdated look.

After. A richly patterned rug is the room's visual and thematic focal point (right). Its cream-colored accents are repeated on the walls, draperies, and lamp-shades. Gold-framed prints and dark woods add texture and warmth to the room.

Two Fabulous Makeovers

The two living rooms shown here both suffered from severe cases of neglect. In one living room, the client's wing chairs and Victorian sofa and chair were saved but reupholstered and revitalized in textured taupe and blue fabrics. The furniture was then rearranged to free up wall space for several bookcases that had been relegated to the basement. Only the neutral carpet was not changed.

Graceful soft swags and drapery panels frame the windows. Individual shades in a white crinkle fabric provide sun control during the day and privacy at night. The fluted drapery rod was painted the same color as the walls, then the grooves were hand-rubbed charcoal black for a custom-finished look.

Two of the room's more unusual touches especially suited the

Before. Mismatched furniture and jarring colors make for an uninteresting mix.

After. The sofa and chair have been reupholstered—a textured taupe for the sofa and a subtly patterned, dusty blue for the **chair. Blue accents are scattered throughout the room, and the dark-toned furniture is a warm contrast.**

client's husband who teaches French: the fleur-de-lis finials and the unique upholstery fabric with a French script design.

The other living room shown here required more drastic measures—everything had to go, including the carpet. The decorator meshed dark highlights against a neutral palette to convey the client's request for a '90s look with a neoclassic feeling. Subtle cream tone-on-tone textures maintain the harmony of this eclectic mix of furnishings.

Shutters keep the windows smart and simple. The sculptural quality of the lamps and stately *torchère,* the *faux* stone and metal tables, and the striking black and taupe accent pillows and tableskirt, punctuate the room with dramatic details.

Before. The room cleared of its outdated '70s furnishings.

After. Neutral textures and deeper taupe walls were accented with a mahogany *bombé* **chest and a pair of similarly stained** *fauteuils* **(French-style chairs with open arms).**

🦋 SMART
Chair Backs

These five classic upholstered chair backs are designed for comfort and beauty. Your selection of fabric—whether textured, patterned, or detailed with trim—will individualize these chairs with your unique style.

LOOSE PILLOW BACK

BUSTLE BACK

An Imaginative Collaboration

Before. Low, unattractive ceilings and a surplus of standard-issue wall paneling and shutters make the living room of this '60s-style ranch house gloomy.

It takes a good deal of imagination to see the decorative possibilities in the "Before" picture of this dark and depressing living room. The client who purchased this '60s-style ranch house called for professional help to completely redo the living room. When radical changes are called for, there has to be a collaboration between client and interior decorator. The client must also have a clear vision of what he or she wants. In this case, the client knew exactly what she wanted—a room with an open feel and a semiformal European, country decor.

Together, the client and decorator first agreed to make some structural changes to the room. They got rid of the paneling, raised the ceiling, added skylights, replaced the windows, built an enclosed patio, and created built-in cabinets and display shelves.

Next, the two collaborators made color and pattern decisions. The results were the luscious red floral cotton chosen for the overstuffed sofa, buttery yellow walls with matching honeycomb shades, a beautiful blueberry-colored plush area rug, and a simple, scalloped window treatment with floral accents. A pair of bustle-backed swivel chairs, covered in a jewel-toned striped fabric, added a dash of formality to the room, while the trunk coffee table provided extra storage space. The client's collection of blue-and-white English china plates were hung above the window, drawing attention to the new vaulted ceiling.

After. Striped armchairs and a floral-patterned sofa share the same jewel-toned colors (left). Blueberry swagged draperies, with triangular accents frame the sunny view outdoors. Blue-and-white porcelain plates accent the yellow wall above the window.

TIGHT-ROLLED BACK

CHANNELED BACK

SEMI-ATTACHED BACK

A Passion for Pattern

Some people are just born with an instinct for creating appealing mixtures. Others spend their lives learning how to put things together in a pleasing manner. To discover the beautiful possibilities in merging different colors and patterns, I suggest you study the paintings of Henri Matisse, Pierre Bonnard, and Édouard Vuillard.

The following two makeovers are fine examples of their respective decorator's adeptness at blending a variety of distinct fabrics and colors.

Townhouse Chic

Multicolored wallpaper dominates the living room of this charming townhouse owned by recent retirees. The decorator kept the large-scaled pattern from being too overpowering by covering only the upper portions of the walls and painting the bottom portions a solid, creamy off-white color. The two differently styled wall areas are separated by a chair-height molding, also painted off-white, that extends around the room.

A candy-striped print covers two French open-arm chairs. A mini-diamond pattern surfaces on the needlepoint rug, which is bordered in yet a fourth pattern. The small gold medallion pattern on the red wing chairs adds a muted, but formal accent to the room.

The fabrics for the flowing drapery and the traditional love seats have additional tone-on-tone designs in white and off-white, but their overall solid appearance offers relief from all the rich designs.

A marvelous mix of patterns in
florals, stripes, and diamonds,
together with a beautiful blend of
solid and multicolored fabrics in
whites, pinks, reds, and greens,
make for a stunning ensemble.

MIXING
Patterns & Colors

Pattern Guidelines:

■ The best results occur when you think of the patterns in a room as actors in a dynamic drama: Make one pattern the star, a second pattern a supporting player, and the other patterns cameo performers.

■ Don't mix similar patterns. Instead of using two floral patterns, for example, combine a floral with a stripe or a plaid pattern.

■ Individual patterns need to flow around a room, blending with each other in an interesting and natural fashion. In the living room on page 81, the floral pattern in the draperies is ably supported by the solid yellow walls, which in turn blend easily into the muted wine and gold patterns of the sofa.

Color Guidelines:

■ Promote harmony within a room by having one color common to all the patterns used.

■ The colors of each pattern should blend together (look and "feel" good together), but don't have to match perfectly.

■ For visual relief, introduce some solid colors to the room.

Formal Florals

In this formal living room, buttery yellow walls are the backdrop for a wide variety of patterns, beginning with the floral design in red, green, and yellow used for the draperies on the central window.

Offering contrast is the generous sofa upholstered in a muted, gold and wine pattern. The room's lively color scheme of red, green, and yellow comes together again in the brilliant striped plaid of an upholstered armchair and in the floral-bordered area rug over neutral wall-to-wall carpeting.

Further evidence of the decorator's keen sense of proportion and scale in the use of pattern and color can be seen in the harmony between all the dynamic patterns and the plain yellow chairs, neutral carpeting, and the soft yellow wall color.

Pale yellow walls frame a beautiful blend of many varied patterns: light and dark florals, red and green stripes, solid creams and yellows. Dark woods and gold accents tie together the elegant assemblage.

Oversized and comfy red-
upholstered furniture, together
with a spectacular zebra skin
patterned rug, make for a joyful
and fun living room that parents
and children both can enjoy.
Bright yellow walls, white trim,
and black accents add sophistication and contrast.

Lively and Lovable

My interpretation of Disraeli's "Life is too short to be little," is "Life is too short to live with things you no longer love."

There comes a time in every room's life when you have to replace outgrown furniture and accessories, hand-me-down heirlooms, or outright bad purchases. Perhaps you don't even need an excuse to redecorate—you simply want something fresh and new.

When it came to redecorating this all-purpose living room, even a change of upholstery fabrics wasn't going to be enough to make the clients like their inherited traditional furniture. With two small children, they were looking for something different, fun, and casual. The furniture had to go.

Learning that the couple loved yellow inspired the decorator's choice for the walls. The bold red contemporary sofa and chairs are another reflection of the couple's lively taste. Built-in bookcases, a bay window, and hardwood floors are recent additions by the clients and perfect complements to the new colors and furnishings.

For spot accents throughout the room, the decorator has added toss cushions covered in a fabric that she hand cut herself to align the blocks of color just right. For drama, she backed the cushions with a less expensive black fabric.

Another sensible touch was the conversation piece zebra skin patterned rug. It has lots of style and wasn't too costly, so the clients can discard it without guilt if they tire of it. A glass table on an iron base keeps the room light and airy and allows a full view of the rug.

A final bit of pizzazz was added to the room when the decorator decided not to use a typical furniture arrangement. Instead, she placed everything, including the rug, at interesting angles.

THE ART OF Angling

Why it's smart to angle:

- It doesn't cost a penny.
- It adds spark.

- It makes a room appear larger.
- It frees up floor space.

How to angle:

- **In the living room:** For a more eye-catching arrangement, angle upholstered furniture pieces in a conversational grouping, rather than up against the walls.

- **In the bedroom:** Place a bed on the diagonal in the corner of a room and create a romantic focal point there.

- **In the dining room:** Try a dramatic change by angling the table within the room, instead of placing it foursquare in the traditional position.

- **For an area rug:** In any room, turn an area rug at an interesting angle to the furniture, creating an intriguing new point of view.

Dining Rooms

Why, when we have the chance to "upgrade" our dining rooms, do we settle instead for dining in "coach"?

I strongly believe in the restorative powers of a beautiful, leisurely dining experience in lovely surroundings—at home, every day. And while we're at it, why not make the experience "first class"? Life is too short not to savor the joys of dining.

For your inspiration, here are nine first-class dining rooms that fit the decorating part of my dream. It's up to you and yours to provide the unhurried meals and the lively conversation.

Heirloom Inspired

In this lovely, formal Texas dining room, the client's inherited heirloom china—a delicate floral pattern of rose, beige, and green colors on an off-white background—inspired the colors of the room. Deep taupe-colored walls became the sophisticated backdrop for the exquisite honey-toned wood dining table, chairs, and sideboard. But what truly sets this room apart is its dramatic drapery design.

Long flowing panels of cream-colored polyester, with the look and feel of raw silk, are smart, classically simple, and reasonably priced. The real eye-catchers are the contrasting plaid swags, chosen to coordinate with the fabric used in the adjacent living room.

A mock roman shade, installed 12 inches above the top window frame, visually expands the height of the window. Braided trim accents the horizontal folds of the shades and gathers the corners of the swags. The iron curtain rod and French key finials were treated with a pewter and brushed gold paint to match the finish on the stunning, ornately carved mirror and on a pair of buffet lamps.

A formal dining room fit for royalty is dressed in honey wood finishes, deep taupe walls, and light cream draperies hung from pewter-and-gold rods. The gloriously ornate mirror and brass chandelier and mirror set a sophisticated, old-world tone.

The Magic of Mirrors

The two dining areas here suffered from a lack of space and no windows. In both instances, the design solution was to visually open up the space with the clever use of mirrors.

Jersey Illusion

In a New Jersey townhouse, the decorator used mirrors to create the illusion of doorways and open up the small dining area. She installed two full-length panels of mirrors, each bordered by dark-toned, fluted wood pilasters (narrow columns). At ceiling height, she placed a bold wallpaper border framed in a dark wood molding similar to the pilasters. The overall effect was to magically enlarge the cramped floor plan: The mirrored "doorways" appear to open out onto adjoining rooms.

Pale walls and carpeting were designed to flow together, further expanding the illusion of space. Furnishings were kept to a minimum to maintain the spacious feeling of the room. A contemporary-style glass table and a set of classic, open-back rosewood chairs add a light and airy touch.

The builder's standard ceiling light fixture was replaced with an impressive metal chandelier, made even more fashionable with the addition of matching taupe shades.

All that is missing here is scintillating conversation to match the sparkling decor.

After. Paneled mirrors framed with dark wood trim that echoes the rosewood dining chairs appear to double the space and create the illusion of open doorways (left).

Before. A tiny and windowless dining space calls for some real decorating magic (left).

Before (above). Elegant Queen Anne chairs and a glass-topped table on a marble base are "lost" in this viewless, dark corner of the living room.

After. Beveled floor-to-ceiling mirrors visually open up this small dining corner (left), while muted gold walls and chair seats covered in a lush, deep green floral print add color, richness, and panache to the charming tableau.

Texas Lights

When this Texas home was built, a tiny, dark dining space was tucked into the corner of the living room, almost as an afterthought. However, the astute decorator-homeowner was prepared to remedy the situation. She knew the best way to create the illusion of light and space is with mirrors, and so she set about redesigning the area.

On one wall, she installed three mirrored panels seamed together with beveled, mirrored strips. The effect was to "double" the space. Now a viewer's eyes are directed to skip across the mirrored image of the brick fireplace in the next room and then travel beyond to the natural light reflected from the living room window.

Six traditional Queen Anne chairs were re-covered in a lovely Jacobean floral print and placed around a modern, glass-topped, marble-based table. Flanking the table in one corner is a large, decorative potted tree.

Thanks to the mirrors and the glass tabletop, now there appears to be a dozen chairs and twice as much light. No doubt the pleasure of dining in this gracious, airy space has also doubled.

➌ SMART
Upholstered
Dining Chairs

Upholstered dining chairs are a
great way to offer visual interest
to a set of matching dining room
furniture. You might even consider mixing Parsons leg chairs
with skirted chairs.

HALF-SKIRTED

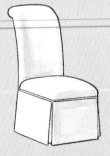

TAILORED SKIRT

Changing Chairs

When you look at the beautiful mix of furnishings in today's most appealing dining rooms, do you ever get frustrated with your own relentlessly matched dining room set? Many people want to make a change in their dining areas, but for various reasons they are not ready to part with the entire set.

My advice: Keep the breakfront (large cabinet), the table, and the sideboard—all the big pieces. But get rid of those chairs! Replace all of them—or at least the host and hostess chairs—with fully upholstered versions. Upholstered dining chairs will add a marvelous touch of élan and comfort to your room, encouraging those leisurely dining experiences we all dream about. Plus, you'll get rid of that dreary matched look.

In the dining room shown here, gracefully skirted chairs soften the imposing walnut dining set in this lovely Canadian dining room. The story behind the change is an interesting one: A wife and mother of three sons restrained her decorating desires for 19 years to please her all-male household. But one day she had finally had it with her dark and somber dining room.

Still sensitive to her family's views, the client hired a decorator to help her achieve just the right balance in redesigning a gender-friendly room.

After deciding to upholster the dining chairs in a simple, skirted design, the client and decorator deliberately chose a neutral, diamond-patterned fabric to balance the floor-length skirts and pretty bow details.

Before (above). Too many dark walnut pieces have overwhelmed this small but sun-filled dining alcove and created a somber and uninviting mood.

After (left). Fully upholstered dining chairs—covered in a rich neutral diamond pattern—and a plush new rug with a sophisticated scroll border, imbue this dining space with a light-filled airiness.

FABRIC-COVERED PARSONS LEG

WOOD PARSONS LEG

QUEEN ANNE LEG

Star Quality

The dining room is the first room you see on entering this new, custom-designed home of a Georgia couple. For maximum impact, the room was decorated with dramatic black and gold accessories and accents combined with the brilliant color of Chinese red lacquer.

Plans for making the dining room the star attraction were set in motion when the oriental rug was selected. Borrowing from the rug's pattern—bright gold stars on a black background bordered in muted reds, roses, yellows, and beige—the decorator chose to upholster the host chairs at each end of the table with a warm red fabric patterned with small gold stars. The seats of the side chairs were covered with a plaid fabric that repeats the red and gold tones of the host chairs.

The "mismatched" chairs, together with the mix of both straight and cabriole (curved) legs on the furniture pieces, follow today's trend of combining complementary pieces rather than perfectly matched ones.

Red-banded silk swags and jabots were perfect, understated choices for the beautiful large windows, and they blend wonderfully with the room's hand-finished, custom wood trim. Soft gold walls above the chair-rail molding are dramatically contrasted with the black painted walls beneath the molding.

Muted gold walls trimmed with a cream-colored molding that echoes the beautifully curved window draperies set the stage for a formal dining room decorated in dramatic red and black with accents of glittering gold stars.

Simple tab-top draperies in a flowing beige cotton are reflected in the mirror above the white antiqued sideboard.

Colorful Country

Hearing her client describe the dining room as "the low point" of her home convinced this decorator that her client needed to do something about it—fast! The client already had lovely, country French farmhouse furniture. Revamping the dining room was just a matter of adding color, hanging draperies, and re-covering the existing chairs.

First, the walls were painted a deep, brick red. Next, long, tab-top draperies in a beige cotton jacquard pattern were installed on wood poles. Soft shades were added to filter light and provide privacy.

The chairs were re-covered in a bright, but refined, plaid. The dark green, wrought-iron chandelier and the two lush, berry and ivy topiaries were the final, sophisticated touches.

This room, once the low point in her house, is now the client's favorite spot.

Deep red walls, white trim, dark green accents, and dining chairs upholstered in a red-green-and-beige plaid, add dazzle and sophistication to this elegant, country-style room.

Dining Spaces

Rather than a full dining room, some house designs include a dining area—often an extension of the living room. What the two spaces shown here have in common is often typical of dining areas: an open floor plan defined by columns, with one window wall and one solid wall.

Sage Brushes

The decorator of this dining space painted the walls in soothing sage green. Then she smartly met the challenge of what to do with the solid wall by utilizing the area for built-in cabinets and display shelves painted a creamy off-white—an altogether practical and attractive alternative to a blank wall.

The soft gray-green of the walls is repeated in the area rug. The rug's custom-made semicurved shape echoes the ceiling curve that marks the entrance to the dining area. A cream-colored border, inset in the rug, subtly complements the colors of the columns and cabinetry.

Upholstered cameo-backed chairs surround a glass-topped pedestal table. Windows are treated to soft, pleated shades and sage-trimmed swags and drapery panels.

Before (above). This light-filled dining space, set off by two classic columns and a curved ceiling line, called for a sensuously formal decorating theme.

After. The soft sage green of the walls and rug is subtly contrasted with the rich cream colors of the cabinet, columns, and cameo-backed dining chairs. The curved lines of the rug and swagged draperies echo the curved ceiling line.

A Study in Plums

Unusual colors and contemporary furnishings were blended to suit the differing tastes of the newlyweds in this home. The decorator started with neutral carpeting throughout the house, but she inset a bright blue rug under the dining table. The blue of the rug is the same blue found in the living area's upholstered sofa, thus providing a unifying visual thread between the dining area and living room.

Walls were painted a deep plum, and the lighter, pinkish plum ceiling color (also used on the living room walls), creates visual flow from one area to the other.

Windows were dressed in a deep, arched cornice with overlaid panels, then adorned with jabots and tiebacks. Finishing touches included an oversized canvas from a thrift shop and the couple's extensive collection of colored crystal.

Varying shades of plum—light for the walls and ceiling, dark for the upholstered armchair— set the contemporary mood for this modern dining room with its floating glass-topped table and upholstered dining chairs.

West Coast Casual

This picture conveys what a dining room should be all about—enjoying the good life. The room radiates an easygoing sophistication that's the perfect look for this large, open-plan house situated on a bluff overlooking a gorgeous ocean and forest view.

The clients, a newly retired West Coast Canadian couple, made a simple, straightforward decorating request: "Maximize the impact of the view and make it an integral part of the home."

The dining room is completely open to the kitchen and the foyer, and it is the first room that catches your attention as you enter the home. To maintain a consistent look in all three areas, the decorator chose a diagonally laid, shell-toned ceramic tile floor for each room. To maintain the flow of continuous color throughout the three areas, a shell-toned paint was used to cover the walls and to lighten the dark cedar ceiling.

Warm-toned, washed wood furniture with classic lines and contemporary iron detailing, reflects the clients' preference for a relaxed, traditional lifestyle. Rich teal in the chair seats and area rug echoes the colors of the nearby sea and trees.

The magnificent ocean-forest view was expanded with the addition of a large picture window to the existing sliding doors. Three panels of a horizontally shirred abstract fabric warm up the window wall without distracting from the view. A final personal touch on display are the salvaged Japanese fish floats.

Before (above). Plans are under way to enhance the ocean view outside this dining room.

After. Light-toned furniture and deep teal colors provide a peaceful setting for an ocean-side meal (left).

Kitchens

Kitchens present one of the most daunting challenges when decorating your home. Selecting surface materials and fixtures is not like choosing fabrics or wallcoverings. The latter two can be removed easily if you decide to make a change. But when you are choosing countertops and flooring for a kitchen, you had better be certain that you can live with them for a long time. Having professional guidance is one way to avoid making a mistake, especially if you are entertaining any unusual ideas, as were the couple featured in our first story.

Midnight Branded with Stars

One Texas couple who wanted a colorful, comfortable kitchen for casual entertaining made a smart choice by calling in a decorator when the building project was still in the blueprint stage.

Clients and decorator decided on the two-by-two-inch shaded blue, green, and purple tiles that cover part of the walls and a sit-down eating counter. Since even grout decisions can have a major impact on the finished look of custom tiling, a navy grout was chosen for its unifying effect.

Cabinets were whitewashed, and the more prominent upper cabinets were glass-paned for display purposes. Neutral-colored laminated countertops, banded along their perimeter in the same blue found in the tiles, were chosen to blend with the cabinets and with the flooring. To further accent the kitchen's architecture and the light wood cabinets, walls not covered by tiling were painted a midnight blue in washable latex enamel.

For light control, horizontal wood blinds were installed over the sink and in the breakfast nook. Mock roman shades with a playful star-studded print complement the rich blue walls, and the gold ties pick up the color of the leather and iron barstools. An etched copper light fixture hangs over a pedestal table, and star-backed chairs complete the heavenly picture.

Deep midnight blue furniture, walls, and tiles are contrasted with natural, white-washed cabinets and off-white window trim and floor tiles for a warm, contemporary look. Gold accents make a glittery counterpoint in the drapery ties, on the lampshade, and on the chairs.

Garden Fresh

Stuck in a mauve and dusty blue time warp, this nondescript kitchen and breakfast room needed a burst of fresh personality (right). The client's directives were clear: Lighten and brighten the room, and create space for a sitting area. Everything except the floor and kitchen cabinets could be replaced.

A collection of cobalt glass inspired the first change: a grapevine wallcovering and border that incorporates the rich blue color of the glass. The original floor was left in place, since it was a timeless, white marble ceramic tile with just a hint of blue veining.

In the breakfast area, the hanging light fixture was removed. A slightly smaller table was added, which freed up enough space for two club chairs.

Borrowing a theme from the garden, where all types and colors of flowers live side by side in harmony, the decorator combined a multitude of patterns in blue and white with accents of red and green. Pewter-finished metal chairs and barstools—reminiscent of lawn furniture—were another reference to the garden.

The window treatment, a crisp navy and white plaid, was kept short and simple, for a bit of contrast with the lighter-colored walls. And because there were two children under thirteen in the house, the beautiful upholstery fabrics were also chosen for their durability.

Cabinets were refinished in a hand-wiped stain that matched the tan edging on the wallpaper border. New installations included a white countertop with a deep blue edging along its perimeter and a white tile backsplash with a fruit bowl motif above the sink.

What a difference planting fresh colors and patterns did to lift the spirits of this kitchen!

Before. This outdated dining area, dully dressed in pastel mauve and blue satin bows, does little justice to the beautiful garden view outside its expansive wall of windows.

After (overleaf). A spectacular blend of warm- and cool-colored floral patterns in reds, greens, blues, and white, combined with navy and green plaid along the windows, draws attention to the garden view.

A small, blue and white patterned rug defines the breakfast bar area (left), where cane-and-iron stools are cushioned in a deep, solid red. Along the ceiling, a lovely grapevine border perfectly complements the ivy wallcovering.

Harmonious Family Living

What can one do to solve the age-old dilemma of wanting a beautifully decorated home, yet needing it to be durable enough to share with the kids? The solution in some cases has been banning the children from certain areas of the house. But a better way to achieve family harmony is taking a few up front precautions that will allow everyone to enjoy a gracious home. A professional decorator can help you "kid-proof" your rooms and make them beautiful.

Starting with the attractive treatment she designed for the arched windows, the decorator of this home made the eat-in kitchen fit for the whole family. For panache, a taupe-brushed, cotton scarf swag with contrasting plaid cascades was draped over unique, fabric-covered rods. For practicality, the window treatment was kept short and away from the floor.

An abstract taupe, teal, and rose plaid fabric—which coordinates with the wallpaper—was laminated and used to reupholster the kitchen chairs, making them stainproof. The table, as shown here, is set for an adult gathering, but when the children dine, a matching laminated tablecloth is added. Another very smart and simple touch is the hand-painted floorcloth, which can be mopped clean.

The parents have the dressed-up look they wanted, but the stress-free maintenance they needed. And the children get the pleasure of growing up in a beautiful environment without worrying about making a mess.

This stunning kitchen-dining area, dressed in lush taupe draperies and light-toned furniture, is completely "child-proof" with its washable seat cushions, vinyl floorcloth, sturdy wood pieces, and off-the-floor draperies.

One end of this spacious kitchen—set apart by a warm red rug—has been transformed into a small family room, complete with built-in TV, generously cushioned sofa, and upholstered chairs.

More Than a Kitchen

By the time the decorator and her client began to decorate this kitchen their relationship had been going strong for three and a half years. Their goal was to make the kitchen the hub of family activity. The client's desire was to open the kitchen to light, and bring back the charm of the 1920s hardwood, Tudor style—and do it with all the conveniences of the '90s.

The walls were taken out between the kitchen, butler's pantry, and family room to create one large room. The window over the sink of the old kitchen remained, but the other windows were reconfigured and placed high over the table area to allow ample light in, but provide privacy from the neighbor's home just 25 feet away. Large windows were used across the back of the room, which opens out onto a terrace and gardens.

The 10-foot work island was built to accommodate a salad prep sink, cooktop, warming drawers, and an entertainment center. Sage- and oatmeal-colored tiles, along with creamy yellow walls, were chosen to complement the natural cherry cabinets. There is also a convenient built-in desk across from the work island.

Across from the white-tiled countertop that serves as both an eating and a food preparation area, a built-in desk with ample storage space provides a convenient, mini-office within the kitchen (opposite page).

On one end of the open kitchen area, a mini-family room was designed around a large-screen, built-in television. An accent rug was used to define the conversation/entertainment area and provide colorful relief from all the surrounding hardwood. Individual, hobbled roman valances, suspended from wooden poles, were hung over the windows to add softness without obstructing light or the view of the gardens.

Clean Country

T. S. Eliot called April the cruelest month. It certainly was for these first-time homeowners when they moved into a 150-year-old farmhouse in the hills surrounding the Ohio River.

In the fall, before they bought their home, the building inspector's report had stated, "No sign of termite activity." Come April, however, the signs had changed: The kitchen was infested with termites. But by May, things were definitely looking brighter. With a monetary settlement in hand and a commitment from the husband to do the work, the couple decided to treat themselves to a brand-new kitchen. That's when they called in a decorator.

New white cabinets were the starting point, then a bold, yellow-and-white-striped wallcovering was used to continue the clean, crisp look. Deep cobalt blue countertops and accessories were selected to coordinate with the couple's collection of brightly colored fruit dishes and serving platters. Box-pleated valances in a fruit-and-vine pattern were chosen to cover the windows. Oak barstools and dining chairs were covered in a French country, raspberry miniprint.

The antique "potty chair" to the right of the pantry was purchased at an estate sale and makes a wonderful conversation piece. Another pleasant discovery was made in the cellar of this old home: the antique porcelain-topped farm table, which now functions as a surface for breadmaking.

Before. A forlorn-looking, barren kitchen (below), virtually dismantled for a massive termite extermination, called for a complete remodeling and redecorating.

After. One end of the expanded (and termite-free) kitchen (right) is resplendent with white cabinets and appliances, yellow-and-white-striped wallcovering, and cobalt blue countertops.

Against a backdrop of yellow and white stripes, a colorful collection of stoneware is displayed in the glass-paned cabinet at the far end of the kitchen (left). An antique farm table, colonial-style "potty," and assorted accessories provide color, contrast, and intrigue.

The Best of Both Worlds

New homes are often criticized for lacking the character and charm of older houses. One Ohio builder decided to remedy that situation and designed a home that features the latest in modern conveniences, together with the fine craftsmanship and attention to detail that were the staples of older homes.

The kitchen is a good example of how the decorators on the project followed the builder's lead and combined the best of both worlds in decorating the home.

Dark cabinetry and hardwood floors have been mellowed with a mix of fruit and floral patterns and antique and wicker furnishings. Especially striking is the juxtaposition of two different wallpaper designs. One single pattern would not have been nearly as interesting. A densely fruited print covers the walls, while a lattice pattern gives an almost tiled effect to the eating island and floating soffit (overhang) above.

More bountiful fruits and flowers surface on the gracious tableskirt, and a mix of seating blends new wicker-and-iron barstools with antique country chairs. The chairs' seat cushions are covered with yet another pattern that adds a lively aubergine to the kitchen's color bouquet.

Mock roman valances in a handkerchief linen with a floral border are suspended from iron rods. As a final touch, a series of decorative plates follows the curve of the kitchen window.

A masterful mix of elegantly varied patterns is the hallmark of this old-world kitchen (above). A rich cream color ties all the designs together.

Cream-colored, linen roman valances, trimmed in the same floral print as the walls, allow for both abundant sunlight and an unobstructed view of the outdoors.

After. This kitchen (above) was first expanded and then redecorated in deep green and maple colors, granite countertops, beige wood trim, cream-colored honeycomb shades, contemporary wood-and-metal furniture, and a generous dollop of earthy, woodsy textures in the marvelous collection of large and small birdhouses.

A New Tradition

This small kitchen needed to keep pace with a growing family. Plans for an addition called for lots of big windows to allow in more natural light. The installation of classic honeycomb shades with controls to keep them up, down, or anywhere in between, gave the clients the flexibility of choosing how much view or how much privacy they wanted.

A lighter, more stylish breakfast table and chairs in coppery tones also helped open up the space. The earthy mix of maple and spruce colors was picked to reflect the whole family's love of nature and the outdoors. The natural look is also found in the forest green wallcovering, which picks up the colors from the green granite countertops.

A collection of unique birdhouses, first introduced to the room by the decorator, now have become a new family tradition. Whenever they are on a holiday, the children love to look for new and different birdhouses to add to the kitchen array. In turn, the birdhouses bring back fond memories of their vacations, as the whole family enjoys this delightful kitchen every day.

Before. This small kitchen has a neglected look that begs for color and interesting accessories.

Family Rooms

The rooms where families gather to relax and play are best suited to a carefree decorating style. But while comfort and ease of care are prime concerns for such a space, it is also important to balance the more casual elements in a family room with a bit of decorative panache. Beauty and practicality can go hand in hand—and should—since so many of today's furnishings and accessories combine the beautiful with the practical.

Splendor in the Suburbs

Deep projecting window boxes between the arched area and the transomed doors in this very large family room presented the first decorating problem. Another flaw in the eyes of the client was the "too peachy" walls. And the lofty dimensions of the room, if not designed properly, could easily overwhelm the space.

A decision was made to camouflage the window boxes rather than go through the disruption of tearing them out. Then the walls were repainted a soft yellow. Finally, the grand scale of the room was warmed considerably by the decorator's attention to details.

A twenty-two-foot ceiling, tall arched windows, and a spectacular view of the woods were all grand and enviable features, but they needed "softening." The view of the outdoors was maintained, especially from the upper level, while the shape of the window was changed by the clever use of fabric. Instead of the floral fabric following the curve of the window, graceful swags embellished with matching rosettes drape down from the center point to the corners just below the arch.

Flowing panels fall to the floor with billowy bishop sleeves positioned over the boxes. Placing tassels several inches below shifts the focus away from the projection to the exquisite passementerie, while visually breaking the long drapery line.

The two raspberry-striped bergères (deep, French armchairs) flanking the fireplace add exciting contrast to the pale yellow damask sofa and white carpet. A generous French country coffee table with storage space below is ideal for hiding away the children's toys.

Before. Unadorned windows completely dominate the room, while bright peach walls do nothing to frame either the windows or the view.

After. Despite this room's lofty heights and towering windows (opposite page), meticulous decorative touches—rich pastel colors, classic floral patterns, and sumptuously detailed furniture—give the space a soft and intimate feel.

The draperies are gathered into billowy bishop sleeves (left) that camouflage a projecting window box built in over the transom. Exquisitely detailed tassels accent the draperies and further distract the eye.

Gently curved draperies, embellished at three corners by large rosettes (above), soften the impact of the larger-than-life windows, but leave the view of the outdoors intact. Pale yellow walls with white trim make a warm and restive backdrop.

The door panels of this hand-painted chest (left) mirror the framed still life on the wall. A collection of blue-and-white porcelain add accent and pattern to the scene.

⤷ KEY ELEMENTS IN Room Design

Texture in the home is conveyed through the look and feel of fabric, furniture, and the finished surfaces of walls and floors. Texture refers to the smoothness or roughness of a material. The way light plays on texture creates a myriad of interesting effects.

■ **Fabric texture** refers to the composition, structure, weave, or finish of a yarn or fabric: smooth silk, nubby tweed, luxurious velvet, glazed chintz.

■ **Furniture texture** refers to the variety of materials used in constructing furniture: wood, glass, wrought iron, wicker, upholstery.

■ **Surface textures** are the materials used to cover floors and walls: wood, tile, stone, brick, carpet, wallcovering, paneling, or paint in smooth, rough, glossy, or matte finishes.

Earth and Sky

The decorator of this grandly scaled family room has matched the dynamic architecture with dramatic interior design. Bringing warmth and coziness to a 27-by-29-foot room was an awesome challenge, but one she met with color, pattern, and a lot of ingenuity.

Her plucky decision to paint the walls a dark dusky green, a color pulled from the stone fireplace, works beautifully as a nondistracting background for restful scenes of the lake. The buttery yellow woodwork frames the window vistas, the large television screen, and the hearth. Underfoot is a cream carpet with a look somewhere between Berber and sisal. Glancing at the photos, one is unaware that the need for evening privacy has been addressed. Installed on the molding above the transom windows are remote-controlled shades that can be lowered to the window seats.

Two walls of built-in cushioned window seats accommodate large gatherings of family and friends. Below the seats is space for games, books, and general storage. The decorator's selection of earth-toned fabrics with purple accents makes a major contribution to the overall warm and cozy feeling.

The game table and chairs, set in a light-filled corner of the room, provide a private place to enjoy a variety of activities.

The richly varied earth tones of the fireplace stones are repeated on the chairs and on the deep sage walls (right). Yellow trim, cream carpeting, and textured, muted gold upholstered pieces, create an opulent but peaceful environment.

122 smart & simple decorating

Before. The original wall of dark paneling would soon be extended by six feet.

Adding to the Nest

An Audubon print was the inspiration for this family room makeover. The client requested that the new and enlarged space reflect the peaceful feel and calm colors of the print's bird scene—which now hangs over the fireplace.

To provide extra room for bookshelves, the room was widened by six feet. The contractor was able to retain the original paneling of the 30-year-old house and replicate it on the new wall by scoring plywood to match. The old and new walls—wearing coats of sage green paint—blend together perfectly.

The open bookshelves and new, built-in cabinets allow space for the home entertainment system.

The decorator had to work, sight unseen, around an inventory list of inherited furniture. A sofa, redone in a tiny green check, black end tables, and crackle-finished lamps were all retrieved from storage.

Simple drapery panels visually heighten the eight-foot ceiling. Underneath, putty-colored shades provide privacy and light control on the west-facing windows, but can be rolled up and out of sight when not needed. The new wing chair beside the fireplace is covered in the same print as the draperies, and its high back nicely balances the beautiful walnut, splat-backed armchair.

The Audubon-inspired khaki and sage green colors used in this room have been carried throughout the first floor, providing a serene and neutral background for the client's lovely family pieces.

After. A classic family room (above), inspired both by the owners' love of nature and the Audubon print over the fireplace, is a peaceful haven of traditional, dark wood furniture and soothing sage green and khaki colors contrasted with black and white accents and floral patterns.

Using Texture
TO ENHANCE
A ROOM'S DESIGN

Rough Textures—
- suggest casualness and informality.
- reduce the appearance of ceiling height or wall expanse.
- make colors appear darker.
- help to disguise dirt and dust.

Smooth Textures—
- suggest luxury and formality.
- increase the appearance of ceiling height or wall expanse.
- reflect more light and make colors appear brighter.
- reveal dirt and dust.

A Variety of Textures—
- make a room more interesting.
- add definition and style to a room decorated in all neutrals.

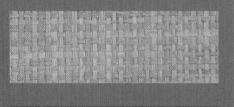

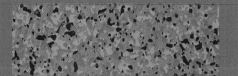

Creating Space

Lack of space—a universal affliction—also plagues the homes of the decorators at Decorating Den Interiors. In fact, their space limitations are even more pronounced, since all DDI decorators have to devote a portion of their home to business and office space.

But when families and businesses grow, space can start getting cramped, and adding on may seem to be the only solution. That was the direction one DDI decorator and her husband were going in, when they decided to change course and redesign their two-car garage to create a family room—doing all the construction and wood-work themselves.

They began by vaulting the eight-foot ceiling with skylights for an extra roomy feel. Then they removed the garage doors to create a wall with two windows. At the other end of the room, they installed French doors that open onto a deck.

The couple's love of boating is reflected in the new decor: A boat border sails around the striped wallcovering, while a rope pattern border follows the ceiling line and camouflages any building flaws. The main colors in the room are navy, green, tan, and burgundy.

Comfortable, casual furniture fills the space. A pair of accent chairs are covered in a "fishing lure" fabric with replicas of a Norman Rockwell painting of a fisherman on the backs and cushions. The room is filled with interesting antiques and accessories with nautical themes.

Before (left). An empty garage, stripped to its skeletal origins, waits to be transformed into a spectacular family room.

After. A seldom used two-car garage became a warm and comfortable family room resplendent in unusual mixed patterns and cool- and warm-toned colors (above). The family's love of sailing and fishing were the inspiration for chair covers, wall border, framed prints, and accessories.

Impossible Basements

It was a tough job, but somebody had to do it: Transform two dismal-looking basements into warm and comfortable family rooms. Two interior decorators set out to prove that each could turn her separate "mission impossible" into a major accomplishment.

Dark into Light

Decorator No. 1's mission was to elevate a dark, windowless basement space to new, sophisticated heights, but keep it user-friendly for the many ages and activities of a family of six.

A tall order, but one eagerly accepted. As a focal point, the decorator created a central seating area within the space to take full advantage of the three-sided fireplace. An armless chair and ottoman and a pair of love seats are upholstered in a solid and plaid, textured chenille.

The warm colors in the fabrics complement the tones in the dark-wood paneling. Restful sage green was selected for the walls and a lighter green for the carpet. A sturdy coffee table and a nest of wicker and wrought-iron tables are handsome additions and extremely serviceable. All of the accessories are strong and unique. They can take a beating, too, and with four children they often do.

Before. This spacious basement (left) in the midst of reconstruction just barely hints at the transformation it will soon undergo.

After. Brightly colored solid and striped chenille upholstery adds warmth and texture to this elegant family room (left). Sage green walls and richly burnished wood paneling are sumptuous complements.

Messy to Marvelous

A similarly daunting task faced Decorator No. 2 when she was given the job of turning a disastrous basement destroyed by doggy damage into a cozy family retreat. With nothing at all to salvage from the original space, the decorator's "mission impossible" was to start from scratch.

Block walls were given a thin, masonry coat and painted a creamy color. An existing ceiling grid received a fresh coat of white paint, and new floor tiles were laid in place. The floor was then covered with a light Berber carpet.

Getting a sofa and love seat through the basement's small access way could have been a major obstacle, if it had not been for a unique system of furniture components ordered by the decorator. Once these individual pieces are assembled and locked into position, no one is aware they were not delivered in one piece.

The earthy tones in the plaid and in the pillow fabrics wonderfully suit the client's collection of African art and artifacts—including the authentic tribal shield hung over the sofa. A windowpane screen is another conversation piece.

Before. One rambunctious dog almost destroyed this basement space, leaving its owners little choice but to revamp and redecorate.

After. This sophisticated basement family room is a testament to the visual power of subtle, neutral tones and patterns (above). The muted beige, cream, and brown colors are a perfect backdrop for the client's collection of African art.

Caribbean Cottage

Was it the California lifestyle, or Tonie, the decorator, or Betty, the 70-something client that inspired this lively sitting room? No doubt it was the lucky combination of all three.

The decorator explains that Betty asked for her home to reflect her age—the age she feels, that is, not the age she is. After a diving trip in the Caribbean, Betty decided to transform her home from an old lady's place into what she called a "Caribbean Cottage."

Painting the walls yellow filled the room with eternal sunshine. An old sofa and chair were resurrected from the garage and reupholstered in a bright pink, textured fabric. Tonie selected a cheerful plaid to cover the chair, a lampshade, a seat cushion, the pillows, and a scalloped valance. The crisp white of the wood blinds is echoed in the furnishings and chair. Accessories reflect Betty's tropical travels.

In fact, it was during one of Betty's trips that Tonie completed the project. When Betty arrived home and saw the brilliant colors of her redecorated cottage, she broke down and cried. At first Tonie mistook the tears for disapproval, until she heard Betty say, "I love it. Thank you for giving me back my youth!"

Before. The owner of this staid and colorless family room wanted a radical transformation that would more closely resemble her newfound, free-spirited nature.

After. In a corner of the cottage's tropical-style family room, a mock, white picket fence and comfy white wicker chair make for a peaceful nook to read or daydream (right).

After. The sunny yellow walls and fireplace are wonderfully contrasted with the bright pinks in the solid and plaid upholstery and valances (opposite page). Whimsical tropical accents abound, and white painted furniture and blinds add a calming—and cooling—touch.

Amazing Grace

Some rooms are without any saving graces. Others, if put in the hands of the right creative person, can be redeemed and given a new life. When it came to rescuing the wretched family room furnishings of a longtime client, the decorator of this room was a godsend. Everything was salvaged and revitalized. The existing cornice boards were restyled into a more streamlined mock roman shade. Underneath, two-inch honey maple wood blinds replaced the old white miniblinds.

Upholstered pieces were reborn with a heavenly new array of textured fabrics and detailed with welt cording. The clever answer to a very large square ottoman was to cut it in half, creating two more serviceable pieces.

The old white walls were repainted a rich mocha, and a range of greens—touched with garnet—brings the room up-to-date.

This decorator's divine design restored the soul of a seemingly irredeemable room.

Before (left). This cornucopia of jarring colors, mismatched furniture, and bare windows and walls needed a masterful decorative touch.

After. Rich mocha walls and trim (left), honey-toned wood blinds, glass and metal accessories, and neutral-colored, textured upholstery with garnet accents make for a stunningly reborn family room.

Master Bedrooms

Before. This bedroom needed light and style.

The "Before" picture in the first story that follows is typical of many master bedrooms. There's nothing terribly wrong with the room, and all the requisite pieces are there: bed, nightstand, lamp, and a once-stylish window treatment. But everything is ordinary looking and out-of-date.

We can all relate to this "blah" scenario, because like the couple who lives here, we believe there are more important priorities than decorating the master bedroom. It is easy to forget just how much time we spend in our bedrooms, but in fact, the bedroom is the last thing we see before falling asleep and the first vision we see when we wake up.

Light and Luscious

The realization that their master bedroom needed major updating— together with the resolve to do something about it— prompted the clients to work closely with their decorator to achieve the glamorous transformation shown in the "After" shot of their bedroom.

As with any major makeover, this decorating coup didn't happen in one day. It was a long "diplomatic" process between the decorator and the husband and the wife.

At one point, the couple wanted to purchase the bed that matched the new birch nightstands and entertainment center (not shown). Instead, the decorator suggested a beautiful, curved and pleated, upholstered headboard. In combination with several neutral textured fabrics for the comforter and a rolled arm bench, the decorator created a sumptuous bed ensemble.

After. Lusciously draped cream curtains and painted walls provide a sophisticated background for the white bed, bedding, side table and chair (opposite page). The green, pink, and lilac floral fabric on the pillows and leopard-skin upholstery add color and texture to the room.

A luscious floral print in shades of lilac, pink, and green was selected for the pillow shams and toss pillows. A coordinating soft sage and gray stripe was used for the dust ruffle and for the large, knotted rope welt on the shams. Another designer touch was a Louis XV-style chair upholstered in a leopard print.

A dazzling master bedroom mixes bright stripes, florals, and solids to magnificent effect. Green walls and ceiling with white trim beautifully frame the honey-gold furnishings and gold, metal, and glass accessories.

Personal Decorating

Some people like to brag about having a personal trainer, but the ones who have a personal decorator really have something to show for themselves. Imagine having someone who knows your likes and dislikes, your tastes and preferences, and caters to every dream you have about living comfortably and beautifully in your own home. And instead of a trainer making you do all the hard work, a decorator does all the work for you.

For ten years, an Atlanta couple had been relying on the smart and simple ideas of their personal decorator. Once they decided to build a new home, she was the first person they involved in their plans.

When it came time to decorate the master bedroom, the couple wanted to keep all the wood furniture from their previous bedroom. They also wanted the color scheme of the room to flow from a cherished painting by an artist friend. An exquisite, abstract floral fabric that picked up both the colors in the painting, and the colors used in other rooms, was the perfect palette from which to redecorate and accessorize the bedroom.

Asymmetrical swags focus the eye on the four-poster pine bed and the painting. The walls and tray ceiling were painted a lovely shade of green defined with white trim. An ivory-colored carpet promotes a light and airy feeling.

For lounging in the adjacent sitting room, there are two comfy chenille chairs and ottomans in a soft, neutral color called "pebble." Here, the Palladian-style windows are treated to wispy panels of sheers on a decorative iron rod.

In a sunlit corner of the bedroom, a cream-colored chair and ottoman, soft sheers, and an elegant glass-and-metal table with books and treasured mementos provide a serene oasis.

A Passion for Purple: Two Masterful Bedrooms

Accents in Aubergine

The lady of this manor, attracted by what she had seen on a trip through France and Italy, knew she must have her master suite reflect the charm and elegance of old Europe. Although her home was new, she wanted all the furniture and accessories in the bedroom to have the look and feel of the past, as if they had been acquired piece by piece over time.

The grand, four-poster bed, needlepoint pillows, linen pillow shams with lavish 11-inch lace trim, lush fabrics, and Aubusson-style area rug, all were selected to achieve a European, old-world look.

What the French call aubergine, a rich eggplant or plum color, was chosen for the monochromatic color scheme: wall-to-wall carpeting with a hint of plum; a deeper plum for the walls; and the darkest plum tones for the brocade coverlet and tableskirt.

Following European tradition, the swags and tails framing the window are lined, interlined, and then edged with yards and yards of sumptuous fringe. A swagged and tasseled border adds another charming touch.

In the master bath, old-world charm and new-world fixtures make a beautiful marriage. The walls are covered in an eggplant-colored damask wallpaper, and a border of lilacs—the client's favorite flower—rings the ceiling. Satiny, tone-on-tone fabric was the choice for the fringed balloon valance.

The deep purple-and-cream brocade coverlet and European-style fourposter are the focus points of this lushly romantic bedroom suite (right). Dusty plum walls and elaborately fringed swags, accented with golden cherubs, add to the opulent effect.

Romance and opulence are also the themes of the adjoining master bath (right). An aubergine patterned wallcovering is topped by a floral border. Bright carpeting and the plum damask wallcovering provide colorful contrast.

Paisleys and Plaids . . . Plush Partners

To move a room from bland to beautiful, a few key elements can make the difference.

When the furnishings are still in good taste and mint condition—as they are in this second master bedroom—the best approach is adding fresh colors and fabrics. Plaids, paisleys, and florals in shades of eggplant, sage, rosewood, and mocha transformed this ordinary room to extraordinary.

The screen print that established the color scheme is reminiscent of floral cluster patterns popular in the late '20s and '30s. Used here for the tailored dust ruffle and pillow shams, the print partners well with a plush, sage green, button-tufted comforter. Scattered on the bed is a marvelous mix of pillows with lavish trims.

Painting the walls soft mocha provided a dramatic backdrop for the sophisticated mix of patterns and colors. The wing chair was reupholstered in an elegant boysenberry, sage, and gold plaid. A paisley-skirted table sits in front of windows treated with simple triangular swags and with panels of airy, textured sheers banded in sage and draped over a mahogany pole.

Completing the dramatic transformation is the placement of a densely patterned oriental rug on the basic beige carpet.

Before. Unaccessorized white walls, ceiling, and bedding do little to complement the lovely brass bed and side chest.

After. Deep mocha walls frame a bountiful blend of paisleys, plaids, and solids in rich tones of aubergine, green, bisque, and boysenberry (right). The windowed alcove is set off with a paisley-skirted occasional table and sensuously draped white sheers banded in sage green.

Classic Blue and White

When it comes to color schemes, there is nothing quite as classic and charming as blue and white. No matter the room, the mood, or the style—family room or bedroom, casual or formal, contemporary or traditional—pairing blue and white is always a beautiful choice. And depending on how the colors are used and combined, the overall effect is always refreshing, no matter the climate or the area of the country.

In this serene and comfortable Florida bedroom, the walls were painted deep periwinkle blue—a colorful backdrop for the client's neutral-toned furniture and white lace bedding. The crisp blue and white Jacobean floral of the accent pillows on the bed and on the wicker settee add pattern and drama to the decorating scheme. The west-facing windows were treated with natural-colored, two-inch wood blinds, which provide both privacy and additional cooling during the hot Florida afternoons. The draperies are simple tab-top panels made out of layers of sheer fabric hung from white wood poles. The petite secretary is accessorized with a collection of blue and white porcelain amidst family photos and memorabilia.

Periwinkle blue walls and accessories, contrasted with crisp white bedding and draperies, are perfect complements to the antique wicker sofa and table.

After. Sheer indulgence is the theme of this sumptuously decorated bedroom dressed in a deep wine velvet coverlet, exotic leopard print ottoman, assorted pillows in stripes, solids, and florals, and an elaborately draped "headboard." Rich taupe-colored walls and carpeting add warmth and depth to the room.

Bed in Disguise

Until now, only the decorator knew what was beneath this luxurious bedding ensemble. Luckily for us, she has revealed the masterful disguise she designed for the old platform bed, making the very contemporary piece of furniture more luxurious and inviting.

After the room received major remodeling, the bed was made the focal point of the room and given a dramatic new treatment. Taupe-colored, floor-to-ceiling tailored draperies—framed with dark, leafy panels—embrace and extend the headboard. Because the bed's drapery treatment coordinates with the wall color, the space is visually broadened and heightened.

The hard lines of the bed were concealed under a gathered dust ruffle and a rich, garnet velour comforter trimmed in braid.

Contrasting red with taupe, textured solids with bold patterns, and straight lines with soft, sensuous shapes makes this an especially appealing bedroom.

The expanded floor plan now allows for a comfortable corner for reading and reflecting.

Before. This boring bedroom (left), with its outdated platform bed and stock furniture pieces, called for an imaginative redecorating job.

➍ SMART Padded Headboards

If you make only one addition to your master bedroom, add an upholstered headboard. You will create a sophisticated and intriguing focal point for your room. Choose one of these designs and have it upholstered to coordinate with a lovely new coverlet and dust ruffle.

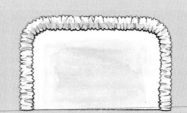

SINGLE SHIRRED ROUNDED CORNERS ROLL

SINGLE SHIRRED CURVACEOUS ROLL

ALL STYLES ARE AVAILABLE WITH A SINGLE OR A DOUBLE ROLL, AND WITH THE OPTION OF A SHIRRED, PLEATED, OR FLAT ROLL.

Glamour Suite

It's hard to imagine the raison d'être behind this spectacularly luxurious master suite, because beneath the glitz and glamour beats the heart of a very practical client. A vivacious and forward thinking widow with a background in intensive care nursing, the client asked her decorators for a memorable room where she would always feel cherished and comfortable.

The room is accented throughout with gilded cherubs and is decorated with luxurious textures in a sophisticated color scheme of black, white, and warm gold. Treatments were specially designed to highlight the home's detailed woodwork on ceilings and walls. Exquisitely trimmed cornices—contrasting richly with golden walls—are mounted inside the window frame. The gold shades beneath the cornices are operated by remote control.

The whirlpool in the corner of the bedroom is surrounded by black marble, mirrors, and gold fixtures and accessories. At bedtime, the elegant bench is used to store the coverlet and assortment of accent pillows. Completing this stand-alone living space is a small kitchen (not shown) next to an intimate table setting.

Timeless decor, richly comfortable furniture and accessories, and beautiful textures and colors promise a bright and nurturing environment for many years to come.

In a far corner of the master suite (above), an intimate dining area has been constructed, resplendent in gold and black accents.

This opulent boudoir (left) is a showcase of gold-black-and-brown patterns and solids, gold and glass accents, and textured and sleek finishes. White trim, accessories, cabinets, and ceiling tie together all the varying elements.

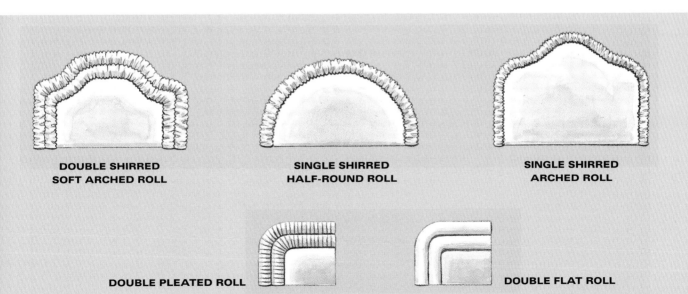

DOUBLE SHIRRED SOFT ARCHED ROLL

SINGLE SHIRRED HALF-ROUND ROLL

SINGLE SHIRRED ARCHED ROLL

DOUBLE PLEATED ROLL

DOUBLE FLAT ROLL

Home Away from Home

"This bedroom hadn't been decorated in twelve years and had become a 'catch-all' room," explained interior decorator Judith Slaughter. "It was time to turn it into the great guest room it should be." Judith then set out to create the much sought-after "home away from home" ambiance of a country bed and breakfast.

A green miniprint wallcovering and border provided a fresh and cool background for a mix of soft, red and white fabrics inspired by Judith's collection of Staffordshire plates—some of which hang over the headboard.

The draperies are simple panels of faded-looking floral cotton, edged with a red-and-white check and bow-tied to wrought-iron rods. The pencil post bed was treated to a lighter, more casual look with white sheer cotton panels. A checked coverlet rests on a plump layering of bed linens.

A black-bordered pillow, black lampshade, black iron lamp stand, and a small black area rug add sharp contrasts throughout the room. "Even a country room needs a bit of sophistication and a touch of the unexpected," explains Judith. "Spiking the apple green and red-and-white color scheme with accents of black keeps the room from being too 'sweet.'"

Judith's decorating plan included essentials for pampered guests: lamps for bedtime reading, a nightstand and armoire for personal belongings, blinds that darken the room for sleeping, a comfortable chair and a cozy chenille throw, and a painted tray table for morning coffee (delivered to the door by the host) that doubles as a luggage rack when the tray is removed.

A deliciously inviting guest room is decorated in classic country style with apple green and red-and-white checks, mint green walls, and a simple four-poster bed draped with white sheers. The red and cream, floor-to-ceiling draperies repeat the same colors found in the collection of porcelain plates that hang above the headboard.

After. New modular units, fashionable furnishings, and a beautiful blend of varied patterns and colors have upgraded this high-school art teacher's home office.

Before. It was time to breathe some new life into this dated home office with a new mix of patterns and panache.

Working at Home and Loving It

Computers, fax machines, and cellular phones, along with Internet and E-mail capabilities make it possible to run a very efficient operation from one's residence.

Whether you are running a full-time business from home, need a quiet place in the evening to continue your daytime work, or want a private area with a desk for hobbies, you will want your workspace to look more like a home than an office.

Each workspace on the following pages is a reflection of its owner's personality. The decorators of these rooms have also addressed the balance between function and beauty by providing for the essentials without losing sight of the importance of aesthetics.

An A+ for Teacher's Office

Babies one and two deferred the decorating plans this young professional couple had for their craftsman-style home, particularly for a more appealing home office space for the husband, a high-school art teacher.

When the time for a makeover came, the couple directed their decorators to create a homey, noncommercial-looking office that both retained some of the original craftsmanlike qualities of the home and projected an eclectic look that reflected their personalities.

Handsome modular units in the same tone as the honey-stained hardwood floors passed both tests. Behind closed cabinet doors is a filing system. Retractable doors can also be pulled shut to hide the computer components.

While the desk and the Biedermeier chair are impressive in appearance, it is their refined scale and proportions that keep them from overpowering the small space. The walls are wrapped in a soft, sage green textured striped paper, and a geometric-designed area rug introduces the color scheme and brings warmth to the wood floor.

Double Efficiency

The decorators at Decorating Den Interiors keep the bulk of their equipment—fabric, wallpaper, paint and carpet samples—in the custom vans they take out on appointments. But they still need an efficient home office for designing, ordering, and bookkeeping responsibilities.

"After living in a mess for three years, I realized one day that I couldn't stand it any longer," recalls DDI decorator Georgia Cox. Once she decided to get serious about designing her dream office, she approached the problem as she would with one of her clients.

Her plan called for two desk areas, storage for a computer, a

After. Cherry wood components were the answers to this home-based decorator's storage and workspace needs.

printer, reference books, and files, and more adequate lighting. The space had to accommodate an administrative assistant and meetings with Bonnie Hinz, Georgia's own decorator. The solution was a selection of nine traditional cherry wood components that together would satisfy all her requirements.

Important to Georgia's plan was keeping harmony between the decorative choices for her office and those in the rest of the house (see Part 1). By following the same style direction and using her favorite blues and golds, Georgia was able to maintain a pleasing consistency between work and relaxation in the Cox household.

A folding screen and fabric-filled baskets give a degree of seclusion from the rest of the house.

Before. This cluttered, disorganized workspace was the motivation for making sweeping changes.

Creating a Multipurpose Contemporary Study

The "study" is the label given to the room one goes to quietly work, do research, or pursue a particular interest or hobby. In the past, study shelves were lined with books, the ultimate source of information. Nowadays, work, study, and research often require access to a computer. The room shown here is designed to encourage study by all family members—no matter what medium of research is used.

Since the study was located at the front of the house—to the left of the entry hall and opposite the dining room—it was necessary that its colors and "feeling" be consistent with the rest of the house. Teal was a common color element that tied all the spaces together. Window treatments in each of the rooms were mirror images of each other, presenting not only a unified look inside the house, but outside as well. The whitewashed furniture, light woodwork, and *faux* wallcovering contribute to the peaceful mood of this inviting study.

Classic styling and bright geometric patterns suit this compact family home office.

Convertible Dining Room

Seeing the dramatic transformation Dawn Williams accomplished when she converted her lackluster dining room into a beautiful functioning office only confirmed that her decision to become a professional decorator was a good one.

When you enter this rejuvenated room it's as if spring has just arrived and brushed away the old wintry blues. Dawn's fresh green palette peppered with black and white accents sets the stylish tone of her busy home office.

Closed, the harlequin-designed armoire is a handsome accent piece. Open, it is a compact office with a drop-down desk and space for computer components, telephone, answering machine, and file drawers. The handsome dresser stores marketing pieces, while the antique bookcase is filled with baskets of fabric samples.

Dawn dressed the windows with delicate floral panels simply hung from black iron rods. The floor is covered in an easy-care, striped pale green and off-white sisal area rug, the same colors used on the wall and trim.

The Williams' old dining table is disguised under a flowing skirt edged with checked ruffles. Comfortable upholstered chairs have been given similar dressmaker details.

In order to preserve the resale value of Dawn's house, she wanted to be able to convert her home office back to a dining room. Now or in the future, when the need arises, this charming space can easily be returned to its original purpose.

Before (above). This staid and stenciled dining room would soon be transformed into a fashionable, home-based office.

A practical bookcase (left) holds baskets full of a decorator's most important tools—fabric samples.

After. Color and pattern have transformed the dining room (above) into a fashionable environment for a home-based decorating business. Office materials and records are stored out of sight in a commodious chest of drawers that helps retain a pleasing residential atmosphere.

Personal Effects

How pleasant it is to take a break from work, lean back in one's office chair, and look around at beautiful treasures that stir fond memories. When Carolyn Christmas, a North Carolina DDI decorator gazes across the room, she sees a chest that was formerly in her grandmother's dining room. Beside it, a photo shows Carolyn at five years of age.

On the wall is a quilt depicting Japanese girls in their colorful kimonos. This delicate craft item was sewn by Carolyn's mother who was missing her daughter—then living halfway around the world in Singapore.

Back at work, a compact wall unit houses computer equipment, and a generous-sized desk provides ample space for that nemesis of interior decorators—paperwork.

The arched window, designed in three pieces, is a tribute to the decorator's wizardry with fabric. The fabric's mix of deep rich colors and patterns is repeated in a wallpaper border that draws attention to the vaulted ceiling. Walls are subtly covered in a natural string paper, and blinds take care of light and privacy.

Soundproofing YOUR WORKSPACE

To ensure having peace and quiet in your home office, even if your family is in the next room or your space faces a noisy street, remember these tricks of the trade:

Install carpet or large area rugs over protective padding.

Hang floor-length draperies, preferably interlined.

Upholster walls with fabric over batting, or hang a large quilt.

In this small but sophisticated home office (opposite page), billowy, multitiered draperies in a deep paisley pattern echo the curves of the window and vaulted ceiling. A similarly patterned rug and wallpaper border thematically tie the room together.

A colorful, handmade kimono quilt does double duty as a decorative wall hanging (left).

Working at Home . . . Sometimes

Kitchen-Office Hideaway

This cheerful nook (right) is a handy place to take care of the business of running a household. Conveniently located beside the kitchen and informal dining area, it offers a pleasant space to catch up on mail, pay bills, and tend to other family matters while waiting for the chicken to bake. With cookbooks at hand, it also becomes an ideal spot for planning future meals.

Clutter is easily kept out of sight in the drawers of the built-in desk, while collectibles and special serving pieces are openly displayed on the shelves above. A wall phone is hidden out of the way under the cabinet but is still accessible. The chair doubles as extra seating at the kitchen table.

A Cozy Basement Office

Part of the remodeling plan for this basement (left) was to create a computer and office area. Upstairs, a door and wall were removed to create an open feeling as you walk down the steps from the dining room. The first thing you see is four feet of stacked glass blocks, curved to cover and define the new working space.

Inside this area are neutral countertops with dark oak cabinets configured for a desk and files. Above the desk, a burlap board displays business cards, schedules, and papers.

A Loft with a View

This loft (left) has become a functional area for homework, as well as a cozy retreat for Mom and Dad to read to their two-year-old twins. The vista from this perch overlooks the elegant living and dining rooms.

The built-in desk is great for doing paperwork, while the plentiful shelving houses the many books, photos, and special mementos of this young, active family.

The "wild kingdom" theme was inspired by their nine-year-old daughter's love of animals.

4 DAZZLING DETAILS

Decorative Details That Make the Difference

What do the characters in a television sitcom, the musicians in a symphony orchestra, and the components of a finely decorated room have in common? Each is but one part of an intricate ensemble. Alone, they are not half as appealing or effective as they are when playing off each other.

In decorating, it is the interaction of various components that produces one beautiful room. Decisions about color, pattern, and furnishings should support design elements such as scale, line, and proportion. Aesthetic considerations for walls, windows, and floors work best when tempered with a sense of practicality. Ceilings—often left to play a minor role in a room—have been known to steal the show. Pictures, pillows, plants, lamps, rugs, and collections of art, artifacts, and cherished objects are the final flourishes that can give a room its distinct personality.

When all the parts of a room are in harmony, the results can be enchanting, as the cozy one-person retreat on page 165 so beautifully illustrates. The warm and soothing ambiance of the room—a combination of easy elegance and down-home comfort—is no casual happenstance. Considerable care was taken to ensure that each decorative element was linked, one to the other, by color, theme, texture, or design.

A *FAUX* MARBLE
TEXTURED WALLCOVERING
WITH A BLUE VEIN RUNNING
THROUGH IT SERVES AS
A LOVELY BACKDROP.

Perfect Harmony

Parchment-colored walls and a creamy white carpet provide the perfect backdrop for the blue-framed prints of gold and blue urns, the delicately colored, finely patterned slipcovers, and the deep blue ottoman. Subtle *faux* marbling on the wallcovering is echoed in the two urn prints. A midnight blue ceiling caps the scene and reflects the many blue accents throughout the room. Natural wood finishes—found in the ottoman's pedestal feet, the matchstick shades, and the frames on the three small prints—lend a light, soft touch to the space, while the unusually hung white sheers add contrast, shape, and texture.

TWO URN PRINTS
ARE FRAMED IN
THE SAME BLUE THAT
COVERS THE CEILING.

OPEN SHELVING HOLDS
SOME OF THE OWNER'S
FAVORITE THINGS.

NATURAL COLORS
AND TEXTURES
ARE CONTRASTED
WITH DEEP BLUE.

THE SLIPCOVERED,
OVERSIZED CHAIR PROVIDES
A COMFORTABLE SPOT FOR
READING, WATCHING TV,
OR JUST DAYDREAMING.

COMPLETING THE BEWITCHING
DECORATING ENSEMBLE IS
A MIDNIGHT BLUE CEILING.

FRENCH DOORS—BEAUTIFULLY
DRAPED WITH SOFT,
CURVING PANELS—OPEN OUT
ONTO A GARDEN PATIO.

AN ATTRACTIVE FLOOR
LAMP TAKES UP LITTLE
SPACE AND PROVIDES
NEEDED LIGHTING.

MATCHSTICK ROLL-UP
SHADES PROVIDE PRIVACY.

PRACTICALITY WAS NOT AN ISSUE
WHEN IT CAME TO SELECTING
THE LUXURIOUS WHITE CARPET.

A TUFTED BLUE OTTOMAN
SERVES AS A FOOTREST
OR AS A TABLE.

Windows

The next time you visit a museum, study the way great works of art are presented. Look at the impact gallery wall colors have on the Homers, Monets, and Turners. Then try to visualize these masterpieces without their frames or the background wall color. Some minimalists will plead that nothing should interfere with the art itself. But attention to surrounding color and detail needn't detract from a piece of art . . . they can even intensify the pleasure of looking at it.

A similar situation arises when decorating windows. Some people are adamant about not obstructing any of the wonderful view outdoors. But if windows and walls are decorated thoughtfully and beautifully, they will simply serve to enhance the view.

You need only look at the subtle differences that the window treatments in these stories make to be convinced that even Mother Nature can be improved upon.

Small but stunning details make for a spectacular ensemble (opposite page): drapery rods and finials covered in the same blue floral pattern as the draperies; coordinating plaid lampshades with matching fringe in yellow, blue, and white; a stenciled "climbing vine" that extends the floral theme along the walls.

The Pleasures of a Window Seat

There are few places in the home as captivating as a window seat. It is a quiet nook for daydreaming, making plans, writing in a journal, reading a favorite book, or relaxing to music.

It was the dream of one day having just such a special place that prompted the owner of this house to save the magazine photo of a window seat she adored. Her decorator was not at all surprised when she visited this client's new home and saw a window seat built into an area off the kitchen.

The client wanted the window seat transformed into a comfortable reading corner for herself while her three young children were at school and a place to watch them play.

Refreshing yellows and blues, florals and plaids were chosen to blend with the client's collection of china and porcelain pieces.

Simple floral panels doubled over short, sheered fabric-covered rods with matching finials enhance the shape of the Palladian window and frame the lovely outside view. A luxurious ensemble of ruffled, welted, and fringed pillows and bolsters adorn the deep seat cushion.

The one flaw to this perfect setting was the rough looking carpentry below the window seat. But instead of doing a major remodeling job on the built-in seat, the decorator camouflaged it with a skirt made from the same fabric as the draperies. The gathered skirt is attached to the seat with Velcro and can be easily removed for cleaning—a practical and appealing solution.

The window seat treatment would not be complete without some small but dazzling finishing touches. Fringed plaid shades dress the brass wall sconces. A bordered, lattice-designed needlepoint rug beautifully defines the space. Asymmetrical stenciling graces the walls and draws attention to the arched window. The dual charms of comfort and chic come into play with the juxtaposition of a country rocker with a classic French armchair.

Before. In a sunlit corner of this yellow-and-white kitchen, a built-in window seat with a magnificent view awaits a suitably lavish design treatment.

After. A hand-stenciled blue, green, and white floral vine arches over the Palladian window (left) and repeats the pattern in the draperies, seat cushion, and skirt.

A variety of pretty patterns on cushions, pillows, and bolsters (above)—including florals, plaids, and a charming "teapot" design—all share the same blue, yellow, and white color scheme.

Framing a Masterpiece View

Two considerations that do not apply to paintings, but must be considered when dressing a window scene, are the beautiful daytime view that becomes a black hole at night and the seasonal changes from the lush foliage of summer to the sharp starkness of winter. Both these challenges were beautifully met in the room shown here.

New England Winter View

Sophisticated neutral tones were chosen to convey the calm elegance that the clients wanted for entertaining. And sensible but beautiful textures were used to set a more casual mood when the space is used as a family room.

The walls have been painted in two wide stripes: one a pale version of the moss green color on the sofa and love seat; the other the same peachy tone found in the patterned chair fabric.

Heavily textured throw swags loop over two-inch wood rods. Repeating the colors of the wall stripes are multitoned wood blinds.

As a final touch, the warm hues in the lovely area rug echo the variety of colors and patterns used throughout the room.

Before (right). Bare windows, walls, and floor do nothing to warm up this New England living room or to frame the lovely view outdoors.

After. The olive green furniture remains but has been warmed up with the addition of a colorful rug (right). Moss green walls and elegantly swagged moss green fabric beautifully frame the snowy scene outdoors.

After. Brilliant red floral draperies, topped with swagged valances trimmed in a coordinating plaid, are hung from burnished wood rods installed at ceiling height. The extra wide drapery panels extend well beyond each window frame, giving the illusion of a wall of windows.

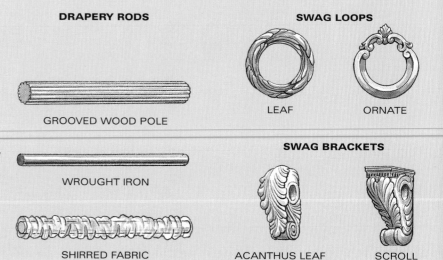

⟩ SMART
Drapery Hardware

There was a time when drapery hardware was purely functional and hidden behind layers of fabric. Now the most fashionable window treatments expose handsome rods and brackets. Swags are pulled through ornamental rings or holders. Finials and tiebacks dress treatments like precious jewels.

DRAPERY RODS

GROOVED WOOD POLE

WROUGHT IRON

SHIRRED FABRIC

SWAG LOOPS

LEAF

ORNATE

SWAG BRACKETS

ACANTHUS LEAF

SCROLL

Fiery Florals

Choosing a bold red floral print was the first step in broadening the appeal of these unassuming windows. But what makes them really stand out is the decorator's design to visually expand the windows' width and height through the clever use of swags, valances, and panels.

The modest dimensions were first improved by the addition of soft, swagged valances on a wood rod installed at ceiling height. Extra full drapery panels extend several inches beyond the window frame. The overall effect is to both widen and lengthen the windows, fooling the eye into seeing more stately proportions.

The plaid banding on the valances is repeated on the pillow covers, adding a more casual feel to this pretty family room.

Before. Standard-sized windows dressed in blinds only fade into the walls and add to the drabness of this dark, cluttered family room.

FINIALS

PINEAPPLE

FLEUR-DE-LIS

SHEPHERD'S CROOK

IMPERIAL KEY

FABRIC-COVERED BALL

SKIRT FABRIC-COVERED BALL

TIEBACK HOLDERS

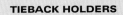

ROSETTE

SHELL

LEAFY SCROLL

Triple Abundance

In a Virginia dining room in a house near elegant Mount Vernon, refinement has made the perfect match with luxury. The drapery design is simple, but the triple fullness of the fabric and the embellishments are exquisitely detailed.

The charming fruit-and-floral pattern is taken from a nineteenth-century French document print and is well deserving of the grand selection of passementerie (see next page). At the top of the valance, thick cording is swagged and bowed along the width of the drapery, while a tassel fringe accentuates the scalloped edge of the slightly tapered valance.

Blue damask fabric was attached to the last fold of the printed panels, creating the illusion of layers of drapery. A decorative tassel trim hides the line where the two fabrics are seamed together. The stunning wood and silk tassel tiebacks were placed low, giving a relaxed look to the elegant train and abundant folds of the drapery panels.

Mount Vernon was also the influence for the handsome mahogany furniture. Two upholstered chairs provide both extra seating and a lovely contrast against the dark wood.

With all the attention paid to luxurious details, this room possesses an understated, refined elegance that would have pleased the tastes of its former neighbors, George and Martha Washington. The fabric name, "Abundance," says it all.

Before. This formal dining room (above), with its classic bay window and a pristine wood-lands view, called for a rich but simple drapery treatment embellished with elegant passementerie.

After. Framing the elegant bay window in this colonial dining room are elaborately gathered and opulently detailed valanced draperies in subtle shades of green, red, and rose on a creamy background.

⮞ SMART
Passementerie

Passementerie—or decorative trim-mings—can be the detail that lifts the ordinary into a thing of beauty. Passementerie, however exotic this French word sounds, are readily available in a wide range of materi-als and prices, making it possible for everyone to binge on fringe.

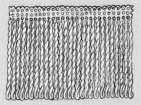

BULLION FRINGE

TASSEL FRINGE

DOUBLE
TASSEL
TIEBACK

CORDING

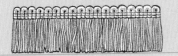

BRUSH FRINGE

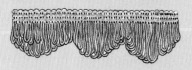

FAN EDGE FRINGE

One-of-kind, silk-tasseled wood tiebacks—trimmed with delicate tatting and beadwork—softly gather the drapery panels into deep folds (above).

The valance is topped with olive green cording that has been looped and bow-tied across the length of the window (above). Matching fringe finishes the scalloped edges of the valance.

Simple Elegance

A long sweep of nearly ceiling-height draperies adorns the soft green walls surrounding a dining room bay window. Muted striped panels are installed with rings on a wood pole that matches the ceiling molding. The draperies' graceful train and double row of tiered ruffles suit the understated mood of the room. Charming touches can be found in the delicate flowers hand-painted at the ceiling corners.

Cascading softly to the floor, the draperies are trimmed to coordinate with the wine host chairs and the soft green walls (above).

 **SMART TAB-TOP**
Drapery Headings

Whatever the design of a room, the trend in window treatments today is less rigid, more flowing. It all begins at the top with simple tab headings. The type of fabric selected and the detail of the headings will dictate the tab-top style most fitting for the mood of the room.

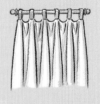

TRADITIONAL

ATTACHED VALANCES WITH STRING TIES

BANDING & BUTTONS

SLOUCH

GATHERED TABS

One can almost hear the music of Mozart weaving its way around the spectacularly detailed furniture and accessories of this sophisticated old-world drawing room. Deep blue walls and ceiling are contrasted with bright white trim and richly toned furniture.

Walls

Whether painted, papered, or paneled, faux-finished, frescoed, or fabric-covered, walls shape, define, and ultimately enhance all the other decorative details in a room. The right wall treatment will give new life to old furniture and accessories, provide a one-of-a-kind backdrop for a special window treatment, or fabulously frame a gorgeous view outdoors. The wrong wall treatment or color will diminish the other decorative elements in a room, no matter how lovely or cherished they are.

Divinely Dark

Convincing clients to paint or paper walls a dark color can be a formidable challenge for interior decorators. But when clients are willing to step out of the beige "comfort zone," they open their homes to the most extraordinary possibilities. As the photos attest, there was no "playing it safe" with the designs in these two rooms.

Mood Indigo

A lovingly restored 1888 Chickering piano sets the tone for this room's grand design scheme. Colors and patterns for the room came from the client's oriental rug. The walls and ceiling were painted a deep federal blue, with the molding and coffers painted a contrasting oyster white.

The opulent composition for the window is an intricate design using a striped jacquard lined in damask and interlined with felt. The perfect proportions of swags, jabots, and panels are accented with luxurious tricolor cord and tassels.

The blue-and-gold, jacquard-and-damask drapery panels are softly gathered into bishop's sleeves two-thirds of the way down and tied with a distinctive, multicolored cord and tassel.

In a quiet corner of the room, the ornately detailed window treatment—an intricate combination of striped panels, swags, and jabots—softly frames the terraced view outdoors.

Vintage Bordeaux

Dark *faux* wallcovering the color of rich Bordeaux wine serves as a smooth backdrop for this handsome study. The Palladian-style windows reach further dramatic heights with taupe, moiré-embossed velvet draperies.

Because the 54-inch drapery fabric had been woven "railroaded" (that is, horizontally), each drapery panel was made in two pieces with an angled overlay. To ensure adequate length, the panel overlays were further banded, trimmed, and then finished with large black tassels. Short pinch pleats without buckram (the stiff fabric used for interlining drapery headings) create a unique heading for the flowing panels. Rods, rings, and finials have been custom-finished in black satin and platinum.

The walls have been treated to a deep, dark-toned *faux* finish, creating the illusion of a textured wallcovering. This wall treatment is a perfect backdrop for the elegant mahogany furniture and the taupe-colored velvet draperies.

Transforming an Ugly Wall

The solutions to some decorating challenges require a bit of experience and experimentation. Interior decorators who risk doing some trial-and-error work on their own homes first, can then share the benefits of their hard-earned knowledge and hands-on labor with their lucky clients.

The bathroom (above) has been redecorated in soft colors and simple accents: cream-and-gold wallcovering, fresh white accessories, gold-framed photographs, and delicately detailed wall sconces with glass shades.

Before (above). Wood paneling darkened and "closed up" this potentially bright and spacious looking bedroom.

After. It is hard to imagine that this room was once a dark cave of mottled wood paneling. A unique paint-and-fresco method transformed the walls into a smooth and rich, muted gold backdrop for a spectacularly detailed four-poster bed. Matching carpeting visually enlarges the room.**

Ingenuity and Imagination

A few years ago, when decorator Deborah Broughton and her husband, John, moved into a fixer-upper house, they selected the smaller of two master bedrooms as their own because it needed less work. Now the time had come to take over the larger bedroom and design a new master retreat in the continental style they had seen on visits to Europe.

The spacious 20-by-20-foot room had great potential, but low, eight-foot ceilings made it feel and look like a box. An even greater obstacle, however, was the less than attractive wood-paneled walls.

Deborah's solution for transforming the walls was to try a unique frescoing method she had only read about. And even though it had never been used as a covering for plywood paneling, she decided to experiment and adapt the technique to her situation—with spectacular results. Her persistence and determination paid off, and after three weekends the pleasant result was beautiful walls with the look and feel of aged fresco.

At a country auction, Deborah found a complete bedroom set, all with inlaid accents and a definite European flair. But rather than use all the matching pieces, she introduced an element of variety with an impressive, king sized, canopied iron bed. Not only did the bed give the room a strong focal point, it added vertical lines and the illusion of height. The striped, ceiling-to-floor drapery panels also create the appearance of height.

Colors are muted olive green and gold, with burgundy accents. Replacing the old shag is a cut-Berber carpet. For accent and interest, the room is filled with personal treasures and travel mementos.

With her vivid imagination and bold creativity, elegant choices of fabrics and furnishings, and the ingenious frescoed walls, Deborah has managed the most remarkable makeover.

The adjoining bathroom was no less challenging, but Deborah and John opted not to do a major remodeling job. They chose instead to work around the built-in dresser and existing tile floor.

A fresh, neutral, fern pattern wallcovering helps soften the angles of the room and cuts down on the contrast between walls and floor. Crown molding is also a new addition. Continuing with the same natural palette is the simple textured window valance over blinds.

A set of library steps is a unique accessory and as appropriate for holding cherished family heirlooms as it is for keeping towels handy. The steps also act as a focal point, drawing the eye away from the massive dresser.

DEBORAH BROUGHTON'S Fresco Recipe for Walls

Combine a Dixie cup of dark-toned "Autumn Blonde" paint with a gallon of joint compound to create a thick consistency for frescoing. First, fill in the panel grooves with the joint compound. Then apply the color mixture directly to the paneling—no priming required. Experiment with the color and texture until you get the overall look you want.

Fooling the Eye

Fabulous fakery has long been a favorite tool of interior decorators. Through the magic of *trompe l'oeil,* a blank wall can be transformed into anything else you can imagine. Where architectural detailing is sorely needed—but budgets are limited—*faux* techniques can create the illusion of stone, brick, wood, and marble. And a room without a view can be provided a beautiful and realistic one through the masterly art of mural painting. The stories that follow prove that "faking it" is sometimes the only way to go.

Fabulous *Faux* Fireplace

This home's English Tudor architecture seemed to call for a stone fireplace in the living room. Unfortunately, that was not part of the original plans back in 1920. The current owners liked the idea of improving the look of their fireplace, but they did not want to make any structural changes.

Instead of the hassle of actually installing stone, the project was put in the hands of a talented artist who created a stunning *faux* fireplace facade that has fooled everyone. The carefully detailed rendering of stone, along with the new traditional furnishings, has added a sense of Tudor strength and beauty appropriate to this gracefully mature home.

Before. This unusually built fireplace, recessed in a small alcove within the living room, would soon go from plain to spectacular with *faux* detailing and rich looking accessories.

After. It is almost impossible to tell that this is not an authentic stone fireplace, but merely a fabulously *faux* illusion by a talented artisan (above).

Trompe l'Oeil Masterpiece

The dictionary defines *trompe l'oeil* as "a decor or art form done in extremely fine detail so as to create an illusion of depth and solidity." Renoir's painting, *Luncheon of the Boating Party,* captured on the stair wall of a charming Canadian home, fits that description to a "T." A painting of a famous French painting . . . what could be more *trompe l'oeil?*

Intensifying the beauty of the scene is the deep red, patterned runner that replaced an old beige carpet.

While there is an overlapping of the "painterly" aspects of *faux, trompe l'oeil,* and mural techniques from an artisan's viewpoint, in the world of interior decorating there is a range of subtle differences among the three treatments.

■ *Faux.* A technique of "faking" an effect or object by painting various surfaces and/or adding texture to walls, primarily to make them resemble the likes of stone, wood, or marble.

■ *Trompe l'oeil.* An artist's technique of mimicking an object or view that is so real it literally "fools the eye" into believing the scene or material painted is the actual thing.

■ *Mural.* Like an exquisite landscape painting—only covering an entire wall—a mural is an artist's rendition of an impressive view.

So beautifully executed is this wall treatment that only the owners' dog peeking out from under the tablecloth is a giveaway that Renoir himself did not paint this rendition of his masterpiece.

Whimsical Wall Treatments

For the daring, adventurous, and downright outrageous, a blank wall can provide an irresistible opportunity to indulge in one's favorite fantasy or fiction, wish or whimsy. Create a memorable wall by yourself, using paint, stencils, cutouts, patience, and imagination. Or hire a local artist to create a made-to-order work of art.

Parrot Paradise

For this West Coast Florida client, the goal was to give her bedroom the feeling of a perpetual vacation, Key West-style. When it came to filling the huge empty space over her bed, a fantastical mural was the answer.

The artist's depiction of a tropical beach scene was given a touch of realism once the view was framed by *trompe l'oeil* plantation shutters. A feline painted on the windowsill pleases the cat-loving client.

A Bevy of Seals

Since this room overlooked the ocean, and the address was Seal Cove Road, there seemed no more ideal subject for a mural than sea and seals. Now this fascinating wraparound scene provides constant pleasure. Remote-controlled shades under box-pleated valances address the intense sun with practicality and panache. Continuing the sensation of water is a low pile, ocean blue carpet installed flush with the white tile floors.

Under the Sea

Walls are painted the color of the Caribbean Sea, and fish swim across a border positioned a couple of feet below the ceiling line (left). The underwater effect of seagrasses, coral, and fish are a combination of hand-painted marine life and fish cutouts from extra border pieces. Playful accessories and primary colors carry out the nautical theme.

Ceilings

Ceilings are often the most overlooked decorative element in a room, usually treated to a layer of white paint and then promptly forgotten. Yet a beautiful ceiling treatment—dramatically painted, custom-papered, hand-stenciled or draped with fabric can transform an already special room into a spectacular showplace.

Tray Ceilings

Most common to homes south of the Mason-Dixon line are what are known as tray ceilings (like a deep inverted tray). Beyond a simple paint color, there are many ways to play up the dramatic proportions of these intrinsically grand ceilings.

A Touch of Exotica

One worldly decorator fused pattern and color in the manner of a Pierre Bonnard canvas to create a uniquely personal bedroom. Inspiration came from her exotic collection of furnishings: a brass bed from Korea and oriental rugs from Persia and Singapore.

But it is the treatment of the unique tray ceiling that is the room's design catalyst. The ceiling was edged with two rows of a patterned wallpaper border and sponge-painted with a blend of intriguing muted colors.

The oriental rugs inspired the exotic ceiling treatment.

A Study in Chiaroscuro

The second bedroom also makes a bow to the art world, but this time by borrowing from a classic painting technique—chiaroscuro. Chiaroscuro is the technique of juxtaposing light and dark, tints and shades. This bedroom, decorated to suit a client's taste, shows only the subtlest of patterns and is remarkable in its absence of color.

Walls and ceiling have been *faux*-finished with a marble effect. Shades and tints of this same color are seen throughout the room and change tones depending on how the light hits the various angles of the tray ceiling. All the trim and shutters have been painted a soft white.

To appreciate the room's understated details one has to study the picture carefully. The reversible comforter has a wide striped border carefully mitered to fit the medallion-embossed washed fabric on the top of the bed. The underside has a unique buttoned flap, turned down at the top. Adding a tailored influence to the scrolled iron bed is a box-pleated bedskirt.

The contrast of black elements and dark wood against natural textures is very striking, and fabric cover-ups over the walnut-stained night chests help keep the dark and light proportions in check.

On the bed, no two pillows are alike, including fronts and backs. This is a splendid example of how a variety of designs and textures, touched with dark accents, makes a neutral palette not only effective, but sensational.

In the elegant sitting area, matching chairs and ottoman upholstered in light gray are surrounded by dark, rough-hewn wood tables and an unusually styled shelf adorned with intriguing art and antiques, candles and memorabilia.

The ultrasophisticated gray and natural tone-on-tone decor (left) is enlivened by a mix of subtle patterns and textures, *faux* marbling set off by white trim on walls and ceiling, and sharp black accents in the furniture and accessories.

Tented Ceiling

If you traipsed across the desert and came upon this tented oasis you would know you were in a typical Arabian setting. But if you were traveling through Ohio and came upon this dramatic scene, you would find it a surprising sight indeed! And that's exactly what the client had in mind when he asked his decorator to canopy his dining room ceiling and make the space look like the tented palace of a Middle Eastern chieftain.

To create a fabulous focal point for the client's multicultural furnishings, the decorator designed an elaborate tented effect. Cording and lavish tassels embellish yards of gathered, taupe, *faux*-finished fabric. The Eastlake dining chairs are covered in a sage green velvet that mixes well with a Moroccan, pierced brass light fixture and a Persian-inspired rug.

When the occasion calls for it, hidden lighting beneath the canopy can simulate the desert sun.

Rich taupe fabric, finished with a glimmering sheen, is lavishly gathered to form a tented ceiling in this masterful dining room that pays homage to the Middle East. A brass Moroccan chandelier, urn-shaped gold tablebase, and stately Eastlake chairs add dazzle and dash to the scene.

A sunbright and spacious atrium has been treated to a charming "natural" decor. Curving grapevines cover the ceiling, creating an arborlike effect for the owner's extensive collection of large and small birdhouses. Potted plants and flowers, furniture painted in muted greens, and an ivy-bordered, hand-painted rug continue the natural theme.

Nature's Ceiling

The vine-covered ceiling of this sun-drenched atrium is definitely worth noting, but so too is the assemblage of fascinating accessories. With its terra-cotta tile floor and garden exposure, this space has become a natural haven for flowers, birds, and, in particular, for birdhouses of every style, size, and shape.

In the center of the room sits a table made of recycled wood from an old fence. The wood was scraped, cleaned, and "aged," then fashioned into a marvelous rendition of a large birdhouse. Handpainted birdhouses were used as finials on the verdigris-painted wood pole that is draped with swags of fabric.

On the ceiling, rambling grapevines are wrapped in small white lights to create instant "starry nights." The painted canvas rug was a gift from a friend, and a pair of Divine Design pillows, featuring a sunflower and doves, adorn the summery iron chairs.

Personal Collections

We can tell a lot about people's passions by what they collect. Most of us start collecting at an early age. At first, it may be dolls, stamps, or baseball cards. Later, a change of interests might lead to collecting plates, glassware, CDs, posters, or books. Collections are often built around personal themes, but they can run the gamut from very general to narrowly focused. Some collections begin with a

Blue and White Collectibles

The color scheme of this lovely breakfast area is the perfect backdrop for the homeowner's incredible assortment of blue and white plates and objects. The white wicker furniture blends well with the oriental flavor of the collection. But a matching wicker piece to house these treasures would not have been nearly as attractive as the unique, split bamboo hutch. It is not only how you arrange your collections, but where you put them that adds drama and style to the overall effect.

few inherited pieces and continue to grow through the years. Other collections start as a thoughtful gift that encourages the receiver to buy more of the same.

Many people are challenged when it comes to displaying their collections. The simple tips shared on the next few pages will inspire you to find your own special way of showing off your personal treasures.

A Chorus of Candleholders

An antique table is the setting for an exquisite assemblage of glass candleholders. But what really makes this group of candleholders special are their unusual colors and intriguing shapes. Placing the candleholders at varying heights, on the table and on stacked books, makes for an appealing still life.

Cobalt Blue Treasures

The accessories on this fireplace mantel change with the seasons, as befits this home in a rugged northern climate. During spring and summer, the owner brings out her collection of cobalt blue treasures, including old poison bottles, found over the past fifteen years, and new pieces by various artists.

Indulging a Passion for Plates

Framing a Window

A common spot for a series of plates is over a window, but in an unusual twist, this decorator placed her plates on the window frame itself (below). Four plates around an oval platter make a pleasing composition for this catch of antique china with a fish motif. It's a lovely way to dress up the simple row of pleated shades.

If you view plates only as food servers, think again. Plates can make the most wonderful wall art, and hanging plates for display is an age-old custom. But we usually overlook this old decorative technique when contemplating ways to decorate bare walls. The facts are: plates can work in any room; they can suit any decorating style; and depending on the value of the plates, there are choices to fit everyone's budget.

Echoing a Headboard

Dark raspberry-colored walls provide a warm setting for a collection of six plain pieces of white china. The arrangement of three small plates over three larger ones emphasizes the curve of the king pine, shutter-style headboard. The room's additional charms come from the cream-colored coverlet and a parade of decorative pillows.

Defining a Corner

Hung en masse, this collection of delft blue plates (Dutch earthenware) takes on an air of importance. The client accumulated them over time on her trips abroad. Intended to be seen and enjoyed every day, they have been placed above a French settee in a comfortable corner of her breakfast room. An extra benefit to this type of arrangement is that it adapts well to new additions.

Smart & Savvy Country Stylings

Like a cute little girl who grows up into a confident woman, the sweetly naive stylings of early country decorating have matured into a sophisticated blend of charm and panache. Today's fresh and refined rooms with a country accent go well beyond the ruffles and flourishes of the past.

Strawberry and Cream

A collection of red-and-white Staffordshire plates inspired the color scheme for this savvy guest room. Papered in a soothing green miniprint, the walls are a mellow background for the strawberry-and-cream-colored fabrics. Sophisticated light pine furniture, white wicker, and simple, tailored bed and window treatments speak a new country vernacular.

Wood and Metal

Another atypical view of country is exposed in this bedroom staged for a Parade of Homes. Sophisticated black contrasted with innocent white creates an alluring background for the assemblage of accessories (below, right) and the collection of rustic chairs. Around the dramatically scaled window is a simple swag of drapery. The ochre tones of the nightstand and the lampshade provide a toasty glow for this country bred, but city fed room (below).

Black and White

Variations on a theme of black and white is the leitmotif of this striking guest room (left). The warm wood tones and refined curves of the cherry sleigh daybed and chest add a touch of elegance to the more informal accessories. Following the vertical direction of the wallpaper are three plates rimmed in checkerboard with barnyard animal centers. On a different wall, a single plate is hung over a rooster print, topping off a cozy vignette of plants, gold-framed picture, and an animal-based lamp.

Enduring Motifs and Themes

Certain motifs and themes never go out of fashion for long. Like slumbering lions, these enduring designs remain dormant for a spell, then return with a roar. Rooms designed around African-inspired motifs or a favorite hobby or sport are common decorative treatments, especially in family rooms, dens, bathrooms, and children's bedrooms. Let your imagination soar and consider one of the charming themes that follow for a room in your home.

Out of Africa

While never totally out of sight, African-inspired animal prints and accessories are more plentiful and available than ever. These compelling reminders of the mystery and romance of a jungle safari can be used subtly or boldly. It all depends on just how adventurous you are.

Jungle Jumble

Setting the jungle theme for this bedroom is a lush, deep wall border purposely placed at a young child's eye level. For practicality's sake, it is a scrubbable vinyl. Lions and tigers parade across the window valance and the bed's dust ruffle, while a unique design keeps the coverlet in place with lace-tied grommets. Even the border on the area rug alludes to the jungle motif. But the delightful custom-designed giraffe headboard is the real scene-stealer here, as the giraffe seems to whimsically oversee his jungle paradise.

Safari Fever

The fearless, pith-helmeted foursome painted on a folding screen makes an amusing focal point for this "cool" white sun-room (left). Wicker furniture and animal prints adorn the base of the glass-topped table and continue the exotic mood.

Elegant Giraffes

A stately wooden giraffe and a pair of wild kingdom pillows make a sophisticated African statement (right). Less bold, but with subtle ethnic references, are the simple earthy florals of the draperies, which are tied to a decorative wooden pole; the handsome pottery lamp; and the refined rattan-and-iron table.

Luxurious Leopards

In any other room but the bathroom (above), this much animal print could have been overkill. But here, the striped paw print wallpaper, spotted fabric cornice and shower curtain, and herd of leopard accessories—all pitted against the white fixtures—is absolutely thrilling.

Perfect "Casting"

When trying to appeal to the men and boys in your life, decorating around a sports theme is always a safe bet, and it has never been easier. With hundreds of fabrics, volumes of wallpaper borders, and infinite sports' accessories, any room can come alive with a sport-centered theme. (And the occupant of the room doesn't even have to be an active participant.)

Fisherman's Retreat

A case in point is this young boy's bedroom inspired by the rough-hewn, lodge-pole bed, and a mother's interest in providing her son with an alluring bedroom.

Setting the theme is a light but masculine "fishing lure" wallpaper, topped off with a "largemouth bass" border. A green plaid valance over skipper blue blinds adds warmth and contrast against the white walls and maize tones of the wood poles.

The wise selection of classic colors and a timeless theme makes this a room even a college-age kid could enjoy.

Rough-hewn wood furniture, a whimsical fishing lure wallpaper, and assorted fish and fishing "accessories" make for a delightful child's bedroom.

Sportsman's Haven

For her avid fresh water fisherman client with lots of memorabilia, the decorator created a northern cabin feeling. A suitable environment was established with green walls and a rough-textured Berber carpet.

To accommodate children and friends, there is a love seat sleeper covered in a rich plaid. The same fabric was used for the tailored cornice boards installed over cherry wood blinds. A dark red chair and ottoman answer the client's request for a reading corner.

The decorative lamps in this room go beyond just lighting the space. A floor lamp illuminates a corner of the room where there is no table. On the desk, the fun fish lamp has been raised to new heights with a couple of books. By the chair and ottoman, a sleek, tall metal lamp—with shade to match—resembles a beautiful piece of sculpture.

Added to the client's collection of antique fishing lures and duck decoys are an angler's rug and a fish box table. Happy at last to have all of his favorite things on display, the client feels that one of his best catches was the decorator.

The fabric-covered cornice matches the plaid upholstery on the sofa (above); both treatments pick up the warm green and neutral tones on the walls and furnishings. Framed fish prints, together with assorted wildlife sculptures, complete the sporting picture.

Assemblages

The difference between collections and assemblages is that the former is a grouping of identical (or nearly identical) pieces, while the latter is an assembly of both similar and contrasting elements, often with a color or other theme to tie the disparate parts together. Assemblages may be charming, straightforward, or downright unusual, as the three treatments that follow aptly illustrate.

Cook's Corner

Against the rich backdrop of a William Morris-inspired wallpaper is an assemblage of personal treasures: a miniature anthropomorphic portrait of a "dog-man"; a framed hound dog; and a copper-and-brass espresso maker alongside a group of favorite cookbooks. This is truly a kitchen corner that exposes the cook's special interests.

Baker's Dozen

A baker's rack (left) is a charming place to show off accessories. One of the elements that makes this selection of dissimilar objects work is the decorator's adherence to old-world colors and themes. What keeps the assemblage exciting is variety, both in placement of the objects and in the many textures—clay, wood, tole, and brass. And note how a marble trivet keeps the angel picture on an easel from falling through the cracks of the rack.

Family Heirlooms

In a guest bedroom (right), a decorator has displayed treasured mementos from both sides of the family. Hanging wrought-iron wall fixtures hold personal collections of photos and embroidered linens and heirlooms, including the wife's mother's satin baby jacket and booties, circa 1917. The parchment-colored walls are the perfect backdrop for this antique collection.

EPILOGUE

INSIDE DECORATING DEN INTERIORS

You have just seen the pictures and read the stories behind some of Decorating Den Interiors' (DDI) magical room transformations. However, despite being an established business since 1969, with representation throughout the United States and Canada, most people don't understand just how DDI decorators work with clients. Either people associate us with old-time, traditional decorators, who can be intimidating and expensive, or they remember us from the past as only doing window treatments. Neither definition describes the who, what, where, when, and how of DDI today.

Who. Decorating Den Interiors is a franchise, a method of doing business that assures consistent service and quality. While each DDI decorator comes under the umbrella of the 30-year-old parent company, he or she owns—or works for someone who owns—an individual DDI franchise. Thus Decorating Den Interiors offers its clients the best of both a small and a big business. When you work with a DDI decorator, you can expect an intimate one-on-one relationship. Yet both clients and DDI decorators also benefit from the clout and experience of a large, multimillion-dollar company.

What. While Decorating Den Interiors maintains its reputation for designing the world's most beautiful window treatments, we also offer a full range of products, including wallpaper, rugs, carpeting, furniture, and accessories for all budgets and situations. Once you decide what you want, the decorator takes it from there, ordering the products, then overseeing the fabrication, delivery, and installation.

Where and When. We come to your home, at your convenience. We suggest, but never critique. Instead, we spend time getting to know you and your likes and dislikes. Then the decorator makes appropriate selections from a DDI van full of samples and allows you to see how various colors and patterns will look in your home with your existing lighting and furnishings.

How. No matter the size of your home or your budget, or the state of your rooms, DDI decorators will be sensitive to your needs and feelings. We treat every client with respect. You'll never be asked to start from scratch, and there is no charge for our complimentary consultations.

Real estate agents tell clients that the three most important considerations when buying a home are, "location, location, location." At Decorating Den Interiors, we believe the three most important considerations when working on a project are, "you, you, you!"

For a complimentary decorating consultation in your home, or to learn more about owning a Decorating Den Interiors' business, call 1-800-DEC-DENS, or look us up on our website at www.decoratingden.com.

DECORATOR CREDITS

PHOTOGRAPHER CREDITS

ACKNOWLEDGMENTS

FABRIC CREDIT

Producing *Smart & Simple Decorating* has been a veritable labor of love. What elevated it from a painstaking job to a personal joy was my collaboration with so many remarkable people.

First and foremost, my heartfelt thanks to the decorators of Decorating Den Interiors (DDI). Without their stories and pictures this book would not have been possible. I particularly want to express my gratitude to Merete Monahan for providing us with the exquisite room that graces the cover of *Smart & Simple Decorating*.

Many thanks to everyone at the Maryland corporate offices of DDI for their support and encouragement. The indefatigable Patti Coons, DDI's Senior Vice President and Director of Communications, was steadfast in her enthusiasm, energy, and friendship. Paula Tranfaglia masterfully helped coordinate the multiple facets of the project. My thanks to Senior Vice President, Bobbie Haseley, for her cooperation and understanding, and to Dick Deerin, DDI's Chief Operating Officer, who provided valuable legal counsel. I am also grateful both to Ricardo Barrantes, for so willingly managing DDI's book fulfillment center, and to my "grand" kid, Jimmy Kirlin, for doing such a great job of cataloging all the dream room photos.

My extreme gratitude to my tireless agent, Ruina Judd, for introducing me to Kate Hartson, Vice President at Time-Life. From the outset, both believed strongly in my vision for *Smart & Simple Decorating*. Thanks also to Teresa Graham, Time-Life's Director of New Product Development, for her input and expertise in overseeing this project. My appreciation to our dedicated book designer, Anne Masters, who has married the words and images of *Smart & Simple Decorating* into an exquisite book.

It was a delight working with my editor angel, Nancy Burke, whose generous spirit and attention to detail added immensely to the pleasure of writing this book.

Last, but not least, I would like to acknowledge all the photographers for their splendid pictures, and Steve Wagner for his wonderful illustrations.